Making Career Transitions

Jane Ballback
Jan Slater

Richard Chang Associates, Inc.
Publications Division
Irvine, California

Making Career Transitions

Jane Ballback
Jan Slater

Library of Congress Catalog Card Number 96-85825

ISBN 1-883553-79-2

First edition

The individuals and events in the case stories throughout this book are real. Names have been changed to protect their privacy.

Richard Chang Associates, Inc.
Publications Division
15265 Alton Parkway, Suite 300
Irvine, CA 92618
(800) 756-8096 (714) 727-7477 Fax (714) 727-7007

Acknowledgments

This book has been fifteen years in the making. We kept waiting for the *"right"* time to begin the writing process. That time never seemed to come, so our first acknowledgments are to Richard Chang and his many talented associates for moving this process along.

We taught ourselves this career development content through our own career and life experiences, by reading a wide variety of business, psychological, financial planning, and career books, and through our partnership of many years with Dr. Ann Coil, a creative and talented program developer and writer.

Our *"real"* teachers, though, were the thousands of clients who attended our workshops and visited our offices with their career challenges and dilemmas. Just when we thought we had heard it all, we would meet someone who had a new and unique story and had the courage and desire to learn something new about themselves and the world of work.

In addition, we would like to thank the many organizations who allowed us to come into their environments to assist in making their specific situation a win-win for everyone involved.

Last, but not least, thanks to Steve and Dennis for their unfailing support of us and the work that we do.

Additional Credits

Edited by Ruth Stingley

Reviewed by Denise Jeffrey

Graphic Layout by Christina Slater

Cover Design by John Odam Design Associates

Preface

Today we are faced with constant changes and increasing challenges that affect our personal and professional lives. Depending on how we address these changes and challenges, they can either be obstacles to growth or opportunities for advancement.

The advantage will belong to those with a commitment to continuous and advantageous learning. The goal of the Publications Division of Richard Chang Associates, Inc. is to provide individuals and organizations with a variety of practical and innovative resources for continuous learning and measurable improvement results.

It is with this goal in mind that we bring you the *Personal Growth and Development Collection*. These books provide realistic and proven advice, techniques, and tools—on a wide range of subjects—to build performance capabilities and achieve lasting results in your personal and professional life.

We hope that once you've had an opportunity to benefit from the *Personal Growth and Development Collection*, and any of the publications available in our *Practical Guidebook Collection*, you will share your thoughts and suggestions with us. We've included a brief Evaluation and Feedback Form at the end of the book that you can fax or send to us.

With your feedback, we can continuously improve the resources we are providing through the Publications Division of Richard Chang Associates, Inc.

Wishing you successful reading,

Richard Y. Chang
President and CEO
Richard Chang Associates, Inc.

Contents

Chapter 1 Key Points

- ⚷ Career transitions can be either major or minor

- ⚷ Plan on about a year of *"homework"* before making a major career change

- ⚷ Pay attention to the early-warning signs that alert you to the fact that a career transition may be a good move

- ⚷ Realize that a gradual, no-risk career-planning process takes time, effort, and a willingness to follow it continually

You Are Constantly in a Career Transition

1

Marvin sits at his desk, quietly tapping his fingers on the keys of his computer keyboard. *"I've got to get out of here,"* he says to himself. *"I'm doing the same thing every day. It's like running through the same dreary maze day in and day out. I need more of a challenge."*

Across the corridor sits Wanda, an account executive who has just been told she's out of a job. *"The unfortunate result of a departmental reorganization,"* she was informed. Wanda has no choice but to make a career transition.

And, on an upper floor, sits Carl, a mid-level manager who pretends that he likes his job, but, in reality, hates it. *"I never wanted to be a manager,"* he says to himself. *"In fact, I don't want to be here at all. I'd rather pursue my dream of opening a bed-and-breakfast in the country."* Carl pauses in thought. *"But who's to say I'd be any good at that? And do I risk what I have here?"*

"Opportunity is a bird
that never perches."
Claude McDonald

In nearly every company, during the course of each day, someone considers making a career change—a fleeting thought of *"What if,"* a serious consideration that balances the pros and cons of a change, or even an edict from the powers-that-be to move on. Whether you're unhappy, bored, unfulfilled, or just plain given the shove, a career change may be in your cards. Don't disregard the possibility. It could prove to be one of the best moves you'll ever make. But do be forewarned—proper planning is essential for a successful career transition.

What Is a Career Transition?

Many people assume a career transition refers to a major change. Not necessarily. We, the authors, in the more than fifteen years we've been in the career-consulting business, have assisted the majority of our clients in making minor changes or adjustments, such as a switch to a different company or to a different department within the same organization.

It didn't take us too long to realize that not everyone opts for a career transformation. Many prefer a makeover. However, with that said, we encourage you to keep ajar the door that leads to a major career change. A number of our clients did make major career transitions, and they were absolutely thrilled with the results.

We challenge you to read this book with an open mind. As you work through it, you will uncover a number of possibilities that are brand new to you and ones that are sitting right under your nose, right where you are. Be aware and open to all the opportunities you unearth. You should come up with a wide variety of them. Why? Because we ask you to act differently and to change your behavior. In doing so, you will attract options you may never before have considered.

You do need to be aware that major career transitions—transitions in which you completely change your field of work—take at least a year to accomplish. That's the average time schedule, and it's the case with just about any major change. A spouse doesn't leave a partner based on the whim of a particular moment. The seeds are often planted far in advance of the actual divorce. Likewise, a cross-country move. How many people do you know pack up their belongings and move without any forethought whatsoever?

However, some people suppress thoughts of a career change. When such thoughts enter their minds, they push them down into their subconscious. There's too much at stake, it's too risky, their spouses won't like it, it's too difficult, it will take too much time, etc. But their thoughts still work on them anyway. In time, they begin to see signs that they're ready for a career transition.

Picking Up Signs That Point Toward a Career Change

We've seen it happen over and over again. Our clients would sometimes reveal different symptoms of career dissatisfaction, but they all noticed particular signs that pointed them toward a career change. What about you? Are you showing any early-warning signs? Take the following quiz to see if a career transition is in your near future.

"Your goal should be just out of reach, but not out of sight."
Denis Waitley &
Remi L. Witt

Am I Experiencing Early-Warning Signs?

Agree____ Disagree ____ 1. I start to feel anxious on Sunday afternoon, because I don't look forward to going to work on Monday morning.

Agree____ Disagree ____ 2. I experience one or more chronic physical symptoms, such as headaches, stomach problems, and/or backaches.

Agree____ Disagree ____ 3. On Sunday morning, I automatically reach for the funnies or the sports page, but then decide to check the want ads first.

Agree____ Disagree ____ 4. At work, I find myself constantly watching the clock.

Agree____ Disagree ____ 5. I feel like I'm on a treadmill that doesn't have an "off" button.

Agree____ Disagree ____ 6. At a work meeting, I seem to be less excited than anyone else in the room.

Agree____ Disagree ____ 7. I don't really care about any promotions at work.

Agree____ Disagree ____ 8. My "give-a-rip" level is low.

Agree____ Disagree ____ 9. I fantasize about doing something totally opposite from what I'm currently doing.

Agree____ Disagree ____ 10. I've started counting the years, months, and/or days until retirement.

How many of these signs do you identify with? There are certainly other warning signs that precede a career transition, but those that we've mentioned generally indicate that you're up for a change. If you relate to these early-warning signs, don't wait. Do your homework now.

> One of our clients, Janine Daus, came to us after a bout in the hospital. As a health-care marketer, Janine found her job to be so stressful that she experienced psychosomatic blindness. "For three months I couldn't see a thing," Janine said. "I was blind and didn't regain my sight until I got out of my career. I knew I needed a change. I didn't even want to be in the same field." She did work on a new career, but it was a pity she stayed in the wrong career for so long. "I identified with all of the early-warning signs," Janine said. "But, to my detriment, I chose to ignore them."

A participant in one of our workshops, a young man, shared with us how he had to wear a special brace around his head for severe headaches that resulted from working in an environment he didn't enjoy. People have a way of developing very good coping skills. Unfortunately, they wait too long to change, because they lack the confidence that they can succeed someplace else in the world of work, they don't think there is a place for them outside of their chosen job or career, or they don't possess the self-marketing skills they need to move on.

Rest assured, dear reader, that we will help you bridge those gaps. If you need help with self marketing, read our book, *Marketing Yourself And Your Career*. It will teach you how to market yourself effectively and will provide you with the words you need to do so. If you're unsure of your skills and abilities, read *Unlocking Your Career Potential*. It will bring your desires and abilities out in the open and prepare you for making a change that fits your needs.

> "Reach high, for stars lie hidden in your soul. Dream deep, for every dream precedes the goal."
> Pamela Vaull Star

And in this book, *Making Career Transitions*, we will guide you along the path toward any career change you decide to make, and we'll show you how to do it nearly risk-free.

But what if you didn't check off many or any of the early-warning signs? Perhaps you're just bored, or maybe you're curious about what else is out there. Are you currently doing what you dreamt about when you were young? Most likely, no. Do you ever have daydreams about what another career would be like? Some of our clients told us they became interested in a career change simply because a television show, a novel, or a magazine sparked a new career interest.

We've happened upon unusual and interesting careers just by being aware of what's going on around us. For example, we were at a tennis tournament recently and watched as a young man pulled numbers out of a hat to see who had won two free airline tickets to Europe. This young man's title was vice president of sports-promotion marketing. We thought the job sounded fabulous—attending sporting events and pulling numbers out of a hat.

Sure, our rational side acknowledged that he probably has to sit down in an office at some point in time and do other work. But what a dream job! Whether or not you're experiencing early-warning signs, we'll show you how to discover such opportunities and see if they are viable options for you. It takes a lot of psychic energy to seem interested in your work if you're really not. Wouldn't it be much better for you if you were actually excited about it?

And don't think you can't make a change just because you're near retirement or because you're tied to a retirement plan. If you're unhappy, and retirement is the only bond holding you to your organization, a career change may be the best move you've ever made.

> Louise Mayberry, a client of ours who had more than a few years before retirement, was facing a layoff within her organization. Louise headed the wellness program for her organization, and she realized, even before she took our "early-warning signs" quiz, that the chaos was not good for her. "Most of my colleagues were hoping to stay, so they could eventually get their retirement benefits. Not me. I went to a vice president, and made a case for putting myself on the list of those who were being asked to leave," Louise told us. "My health was at stake." She was given a very minor retirement package, set up her own business as a wellness consultant for corporations, and is much more content.

However, you may be happy enough where you are to put in time to reap your retirement rewards. But after you retire, if the benefits don't wholly suffice or you aren't ready to give up on the working world, use this book to prepare for your first retirement career. One of our clients, Betty Harris, worked for a company that was downsizing. Since Betty was in her early fifties, her company offered her an early retirement, and she took them up on it. Betty and her husband started their own travel agency, and now they work at their agency and get to travel around the world.

> A participant in one of our workshops, Carol Springfield, knew she had to work after she took an early retirement from her job in human resources. Carol decided that she wanted to utilize her sales and promotion skills in her new career, whatever it would be. "I was talking to the woman who owned the dry-cleaning shop I frequented," Carol shared, "and she told me she also owned a bridal shop in the same strip mall. She was looking for someone to run the shop and asked me if I wanted to be her partner and run the shop for her." Carol did. "I knew from your workshops to be open to opportunities," she said, "and I looked into it, and am now very happy."

Choosing a retirement career is not a choice many people think they'll have to make, but it's quickly gaining in importance. Why? It's difficult to actually pinpoint a retirement age nowadays. Military and law-enforcement employees often retire in their middle to late forties, and a major employer we know of just announced an early-out retirement program for employees as young as forty-seven. On the other hand, many people still use sixty-five as a marker for retirement, and some people never retire.

We tell our clients to look at retirement as a way to expand their opportunities. People plan retirement careers for several reasons. First and foremost is that people want to remain active, involved, and mentally and intellectually stimulated. People also want to try out careers that they always only dreamed about, but never had the time or resources or the courage to do. And last, of course, are financial reasons, which range all the way from putting food on the table to planning elaborate trips.

We see no need to go into a detailed discussion of financial planning for retirement. It's a complex subject, and other people have handled it very well. But we'd like to inject one note of caution: most of our clients underestimate how long they will live and what it will cost if they live much past seventy years of age.

Don't fall into the same trap. It's the biggest mistake people make when doing their retirement planning. Experts are now predicting that when the major diseases are conquered, our life expectancy could be as long as 120 or even 130 years. Some of our clients are shocked by this realization.

Even if you aren't anywhere near the age you deem *"retirement age,"* keep in mind that you should plan for a retirement career. In actuality, planning a retirement career can be an exciting venture. You can be open to many different choices. How so? Well, if you are free from financial constraints, then you are free to look at careers you never really considered before because they didn't pay enough for what you thought you needed. You're also free from other people's expectations about what you should do. And, most importantly, you're free from your own expectations about what you should do versus what you really always wanted to do. An added plus is that you're also free to work less, work different hours, or choose a totally different schedule.

> *A client of ours who was nearing retirement age worked in information systems for a major food corporation in the process of downsizing. He was offered the option of taking a small, early retirement, which afforded him a limited income. His first thought was to immediately pursue another career in information systems, although that wasn't what he really wanted to do. We asked him, "What makes you happiest? What makes you alive? Where would you like to be?" His response? "Anaheim stadium." He wanted to be an usher there, so he could watch the games. On the weekends, this gentleman also taught flying at a local airport. Combining the two jobs supplemented his retirement income sufficiently, and he was happy in his retirement career.*

The planning and labor market research for retirement careers is the same as for other career choices, except that it usually happens over a longer period of time. In Chapter Seven of this book, we'll give a plan of action for a retirement career and let you take a peek at the journal of one of our clients who was looking to choose a retirement career.

The Way It Was and the Way It Is

Not too many years ago, career changes were looked upon with some suspicion. People got worried when they had more than a couple of jobs on their resume. *"What are people going to think I'm doing?"* they asked. There wasn't much societal support for those who wanted to change careers. Whatever you chose for your first career often ended up as your life's work.

Thank goodness it's not the same now. If you decide that a career is not to your liking, you don't have to worry about people shaking their heads and wondering what your problem is. For some people, it's not even that they don't like their jobs. They've just played their jobs to the hilt, and there's nothing left.

They've done everything they can do in their careers—they've gotten all the promotions, and they've risen as high as possible. There are no more hurdles to jump, no more projects to complete, no more presentations to give. They've done it all. We're not saying they didn't enjoy the years they invested; it's just that there is no more challenge.

In the old days, a career transition would be out of the question for these folks. They'd stay in their same careers, burnt out but still hanging on. We want you to know that you don't have to settle for something that doesn't bring you joy, give you a challenge, or provide you with new learning opportunities. You can reach new heights in a different career.

Jerry Malten, a client of ours, was an educator who had a Ph.D. Jerry spent some years in the classroom, and then went on to become a principal. "After that, I became involved in staff development for my school district," Jerry explained, "and then I consulted on a national level with other school districts to help them. Finally, I was finished. There was nothing more of interest for me in the field of public education." We helped him explore his options. He still loved training, and he enjoyed standing up in front of an audience. Jerry left the public-education sector and went on the road as a teacher and trainer for a national seminar company.

Wanted: A Gradual, No-Risk Career Transition

If you're afraid of leaving familiar territory or taking on a challenge you don't want, we'll settle your nerves here. Our approach to career transitions is like a gentle leap to firm ground, not a haphazard jump off the nearest cliff. Granted, our approach does take some time, but it's worth the effort.

If you're in a great deal of career pain, and the warning signs are in full force, you can put all your effort into making a career transition and speed up the change. If you're just bored, a little unhappy, or a bit curious, follow the process at whatever pace is comfortable to you. Just be sure to follow it consistently. Being open to new careers or new job opportunities is a great habit to pick up.

Some of our clients think that once they make a major career change, they can stop. We don't think that's a good idea. People don't stay in one career forever. What interests you now may not in five or ten years.

"Better to get a stiff neck from aiming too high than a hunch back from aiming too low."
Jacques Chancel

We'd like you to take the following self assessment so that you can determine how ready you are for a change. Does the thought of your job still bring feelings of warmth, or does it leave you cold? This assessment will help you pinpoint which parts of your current job or career you like, and which parts you dislike. You'll know what you should look for in a new career, and what you'd rather leave behind.

What Is My Career Temperature?

Apply each statement to your current job or career by placing a check mark in the appropriate space.

1. Opportunity to use the skills I enjoy

   ____Very Satisfied ____Satisfied ____Somewhat Satisfied ____Dissatisfied ____Very Dissatisfied

2. Demands work makes on my time

   ____Very Satisfied ____Satisfied ____Somewhat Satisfied ____Dissatisfied ____Very Dissatisfied

3. A salary which reflects my contribution to my organization

   ____Very Satisfied ____Satisfied ____Somewhat Satisfied ____Dissatisfied ____Very Dissatisfied

4. A benefits package that meets my needs

   ____Very Satisfied ____Satisfied ____Somewhat Satisfied ____Dissatisfied ____Very Dissatisfied

5. Clothes and image that are required for my job

   ____Very Satisfied ____Satisfied ____Somewhat Satisfied ____Dissatisfied ____Very Dissatisfied

6. Opportunity to interact with people I enjoy

   ____Very Satisfied ____Satisfied ____Somewhat Satisfied ____Dissatisfied ____Very Dissatisfied

7. Quiet time to immerse myself in data

   ____Very Satisfied ____Satisfied ____Somewhat Satisfied ____Dissatisfied ____Very Dissatisfied

8. Opportunity to grow and develop

   ____Very Satisfied ____Satisfied ____Somewhat Satisfied ____Dissatisfied ____Very Dissatisfied

9. An environment that I enjoy going to every day

   ____Very Satisfied ____Satisfied ____Somewhat Satisfied ____Dissatisfied ____Very Dissatisfied

10. Opportunity to apply my creativity

    ____Very Satisfied ____Satisfied ____Somewhat Satisfied ____Dissatisfied ____Very Dissatisfied

11. The amount of status and prestige attached to my job

    ____Very Satisfied ____Satisfied ____Somewhat Satisfied ____Dissatisfied ____Very Dissatisfied

12. The match between my value system and that of my organization

    ____Very Satisfied ____Satisfied ____Somewhat Satisfied ____Dissatisfied ____Very Dissatisfied

13. Flexibility in setting my own schedule

    ____Very Satisfied ____Satisfied ____Somewhat Satisfied ____Dissatisfied ____Very Dissatisfied

14. The long-term prospects of my job and/or field of work

    ____Very Satisfied ____Satisfied ____Somewhat Satisfied ____Dissatisfied ____Very Dissatisfied

15. The challenges and learning opportunities afforded by my job and/or field of work

    ____Very Satisfied ____Satisfied ____Somewhat Satisfied ____Dissatisfied ____Very Dissatisfied

Your response to this assessment is totally individual; that's why there's no answer key. You may be strongly satisfied with all points except one and still consider your *"career temperature"* to be cold, or you may be very dissatisfied with four or five points and yet feel a great deal of warmth toward your career choice. So look at each of the statements and especially pay attention to those you marked *"very satisfied"* or *"very dissatisfied."* How important are these factors? If *"very dissatisfied,"* can you change them within your present career to increase your career temperature?

Mary Gonzalez, one of our clients who was a nurse, took our assessment and discovered that she was dissatisfied with the skills she was using and the people she had to work with. *"I really don't enjoy working with grumpy patients at the hospital,"* she told us. Yet Mary did enjoy the environment and the field, and she didn't want to leave behind what she had learned. After Mary looked into a number of different careers in the hospital setting, she landed a position in staff development. *"I love working with the nurses and training them,"* she said. *"And the change I made upped my career temperature considerably."*

Another client, John Strep, discovered that he disliked his management career, primarily because he didn't appreciate the demands on his time and because he wasn't allowed any quiet time to work with data. *"I wanted to spend more time with my two boys,"* John shared, *"and I decided I needed to make a move soon, before they grew up."* John chose an engineering job closer to home. He made less money but was rewarded with more time and joy, both missing in his old job.

"The moment you realize you have more reasons for not going to work than going is a critical moment indeed. Seize it, and move forward."
Anonymous

> *One of our clients, Bob Jackson, made a major career change once he discovered that his current choice was absolutely wrong for him. Bob, a manager of workers on oil derricks, took our self assessment and marked "very dissatisfied" on nearly every item. "My career temperature was about as cold as you could get. I didn't like the environment, the people, what I did, etc., etc.," he said. What Bob had always wanted to be was a chef. Since his children were grown and he had some money saved, Bob decided to attend a well-known cooking school. Eighteen months later, he was working as a happy, successful chef at a nearby resort.*

If you've decided to make a change now or are thinking about the possibility, this book will show you which direction to take to ensure a nearly risk-free career transition. Stick with us. We'll show you more of what we have in mind in the next chapter.

From

To

Summary

Very few people are exempt from thoughts about a career transition. Sooner or later most people search for a new career or job. Whether or not it's sooner depends upon how many early-warning signs you're receiving, how bored or unhappy you are, and/or how in tune you are with your true desires. Follow our path toward a gradual, no-risk career change, and you'll minimize the pitfalls and maximize your results.

Chapter 2 Key Points

🔑 If you create a career vision that takes into consideration your skills, abilities, and desires, you virtually guarantee a successful career transition

🔑 You'll get to choose the strategies you prefer for finding your vision and making it a reality

🔑 If you're already out of work, find a *"hold-me-over"* job to provide an income while you work on your career transition

🔑 To uncover the career or job that's right for you, you must conduct labor market research and continually ask the three questions that put each prospective job into perspective:

  ♦ Do I want—or desire—to do this?

  ♦ What does it pay?

  ♦ What is the demand for it, now and in the future?

You Might Not Get There If You Don't Know Where You Are Going

2

Please don't expect us to tell you what you should be, where you should work, or what career transition to make. Some of our clients sit down in our office, explain what they don't like about their current jobs, and then wait for us to tell them what to do. We're not fortune tellers. Unearthing the right career choice is a discovery process that you have to spearhead. We'll show you what to do and offer you suggestions, but we can't do it for you.

If you've read our book, *Unlocking Your Career Potential,* you're already on top of things. You'll have identified your desires, skills, and abilities, and have a clearer picture of what you want to do. If you haven't, don't despair. Completing the self assessment in chapter one *("What Is My Career Temperature?")* will at least put you a step ahead of others who have no clue as to what they would like out of a job or career. It's a definite start toward identifying your career vision.

> *Mary Nettles, a participant in one of our workshops, illustrated for us the importance of knowing yourself before you start the career-transition process. A college teacher who wanted to make a career change, Mary thought it was who you knew that was of supreme importance. "My husband is a doctor," she said, "and knew a variety of prominent business people. He started to introduce me to them, and I had a series of lunches with different individuals." Mary found that people were more than willing to introduce her to others and tell her about opportunities in their companies. "But I realized that I was spinning my wheels. I didn't know what I wanted to do. And until I had determined that, all the people in the world couldn't help me."*

Why Create a Career Vision

We're often asked how we motivate people to undertake a career transition which, after all, takes time and the ability to initiate and withstand change. Our answer? We don't have to motivate anybody. First of all, our clients often come to us in such career pain that they're willing to do almost anything to change careers. And second, the process we show them allows them to see where they're going. Once they have a vision of where they belong, we often have to jump out of the way. They see the end result and want to get there.

People who don't make career changes, when it's clear they should, fail to make a move because they can't see where they're going. No one is willing to step off a cliff into a black abyss of uncertainty. Wouldn't you much rather have a picture of your final destination?

One of our clients, Barbara Potter, an administrative assistant at a real estate company located in Los Angeles, was interested in a career change that would use her meetings-and-events-planning skills. She heard about a career called "destination management" from her sister-in-law, whose good friend worked in the field. People in destination management arrange all the events for professional groups that come to town. "The job sounded fascinating to me," Barbara said, "but I did as you asked, and checked it out first. My sister-in-law arranged to have her friend, Joanne, take me with her for a day to try out the career. The American Medical Association was to have a major convention in town, and Joanne said she'd show me the ropes." On the planned day, Barbara and Joanne were to pick up the president of the AMA and two board members, who were arriving a day in advance to check out the situation. "We chartered a limousine and picked up our guests," Barbara recounted. "Then we took them to their hotel, brought them to a nice restaurant for lunch to do final planning and preparation, and toured the hotel. Immediately after that, we picked up other clients who were flying in, and took them to dinner to try out a restaurant as a possible site for their upcoming conference." At the end of the day, Barbara was absolutely convinced that she wanted to be part of a destination-management team. She had a vision as to where she wanted to go with her skills. She still had to figure out how to get into this field (which is part of the process we will describe later), but she now knew where she was going and was definitely motivated to get there.

"A goal is a dream with a deadline."
Anonymous

Selecting Strategies to Help You Find a Vision

What we'll be giving you in the chapters ahead are techniques and strategies to help you find your vision and figure out how to make it become a reality. You will be choosing strategies based on the time you want to spend on the process and how comfortable you feel with each. A word of warning, though—you will need to leave your zone of comfort in order to make a change. We'd be lying to you if we told you otherwise. But because you complete the process baby step by baby step, by the time you have gotten through all the steps, the whole process seems less threatening.

However, you may be wondering if you can make a successful career transition if you are unemployed or will be out of a job very soon. It's highly unlikely. You will need an income for a **minimum** of three to six months to make a career change that works for you. If you don't *(and many of our clients don't have that kind of money)*, we encourage you to get a *"hold-me-over"* job.

A *"hold-me-over"* job is any job that is plentiful, similar to a job you've held before, and/or a job you know you can get. It's not the job of your dreams. Its purpose is to hold you over until you make your career transition—it pays the bills and buys you time to follow our process. You've probably held many *"hold-me-over"* jobs in your lifetime. You just didn't realize that's what they were called.

The only danger with *"hold-me-over"* jobs is that they are comfortable. It's easy to get stuck in them. That's the biggest fear our clients have. They think they'll have to keep their *"hold-me-over"* jobs for the rest of their lives. But they don't. Yes, we know of people who have had twenty-year *"hold-me-over"* jobs, but you won't be one of them. You have to make a conscious decision to keep the job only for as long as it takes to follow the steps of our process. Then, when you begin the job or career of your choice, you can quit.

Many of our clients are relieved when they hear this. *"Go ahead and take the job your brother-in-law offered,"* we say. *"You don't have to be stuck in it forever."* Just find one that doesn't make great demands on your time or require travel that takes you away from your *"career-transition"* research. Many clients choose decent-paying, nighttime jobs that free up their daylight business hours for research.

> *One of the participants in our workshops, Rolanda Smith, was a secretary who had recently been laid off from her job. "I had two weeks pay to my name," she shared with us. Rolanda was just finishing her college degree, and had identified that she wanted to be in training and development. "I didn't have time to complete all of your steps in two weeks," Rolanda said, "so I looked around and found a position as a training coordinator in a training department at a major corporation." She was in charge of setting up all the classrooms and scheduling the instructors, etc. It was a wonderful "hold-me-over" job, because it paid the bills and put her in a department that she eventually wanted to transition into. "I started to employ all the steps to become a trainer. After six months, an entry-level training position became available, and I got the job."*

"People who love what they're doing are in the best position."
Anonymous

Understanding Labor Market Research

We refer to the strategies you'll be choosing and the research you will be doing as labor market research. It's a whole host of techniques for getting out and researching trends in the world of work. We'll explain how to conduct labor market research in the next two chapters. For now, it's essential that you understand the three questions that labor market research answers. These questions are placed in a specific order for a very specific reason.

As you conduct your labor market research, you will keep uppermost in your mind the following three key questions:

1. Does this job or field interest me? (*Do I want—or desire— to do this?*)
2. What does this job or field pay?
3. What's the demand for this career field, now and in the future?

We often tell our clients to think of the questions as DPD— desire, pay, and demand. Why are they in this order? All are important, but if you can't answer yes to number one, the desire question, it doesn't matter how you answer numbers two and three. It makes no difference if the job pays $100,000 a year and will be in demand for the next fifty years. If you don't desire to do it, you won't care how much it pays or how much it's in demand.

For example, many people who get laid off from administrative assistant positions (*who know how to type or word process*) make an immediate decision that they want to go to court reporting school. It's a career that pays exceptionally well. Working four days a week, they can make $50,000 to $60,000 a year. It's also very much in demand. But the fact is that unless you figure out that this career is something you'd enjoy doing, the other two pieces of information are absolutely meaningless.

> "The path to your dreams is outside your door. Step on out and take a stroll."
> Anonymous

We've had clients who, prior to coming to us, enrolled in court reporting school, invested time and money, and ended up dropping out. It's not an easy occupation. Had these clients done their labor market research, they never would have enrolled in the first place.

> *We worked with the employees of a very large company that was laying off a number of their workers. These employees had been working out in the field, interacting with customers on their own time schedules. Now they were given a choice. They could either leave the company or work inside, hooked up to a phone and computer, fielding customer-service complaints for eight hours a day. Because they would be hooked up to phones, they would even have to get permission for bathroom breaks. We warned many of them to not even start the customer-service school. It would be grueling, and their new job would be so different from their old one. Every single one of them who disregarded our advice and started the school, dropped out once they saw the reality of the job.*

We have to direct clients to follow our instructions regarding the three questions to the letter. Many people still think that if the answers to numbers two and three are good enough, it doesn't matter what the answer to number one is. Wrong! Answer them in the correct order—desire, pay, and demand. There's no way around it.

In labor market research, you have to get out and see what the job entails. Only then can you really answer the first question. How do you know that you desire to do something unless you know what's involved?

Some career counselors suggest going to the library and plodding through the *Dictionary of Occupational Titles* to get an idea of what you might want to do. If you have insomnia, it's a good idea. The *Dictionary of Occupational Titles* is a huge tome, published by the government, and it attempts to cover every single job that exists. For example, one of the job titles listed in that dictionary is: Sex Sensor. During our workshops, we write this title on a flip chart and tell participants it's in demand and pays about $35,000 a year. Some of our participants get pretty excited, thinking it could be a career they'd like to pursue. Until, that is, we tell them what it really entails. A sex sensor is a person who senses the sex of baby chicks by looking at the color of their beaks.

Have we made our point? The world of work cannot be discovered by reading job titles in a book. Jobs or careers need to be experienced, talked about, and touched. Only then can you create a vision, go after it, and make a successful career transition.

Summary

By now, you've realized that if you want a successful career transition, you have to know yourself, create a vision, and take steps toward making it a reality. And, if you're currently out of work, you'll need to find a *"hold-me-over"* job to keep your finances in good health while you travel from the starting point to your final destination. The journey involves labor market research, which entails an exploration of various jobs or careers, all the while keeping three questions foremost in your mind: *"Do I have the desire to do this?," "What does it pay?,"* and *"What is the demand for this job?" (Desire-Pay-Demand).* Always answer number one first; and, if the answer is yes, ask the other two questions. It's a proven way to find a career you'll be happy you chose.

Chapter 3 Key Points

🗝 The steps of labor market research are similar to the rings of a bull's-eye; the first, outside steps are easier and lead toward the more difficult one that's closest to making a career transition

🗝 You can complete the career-transition process in as little as three months or as long as three years; the speed of your progress is up to you and is dependent upon your situation

🗝 The first and easiest step involves reading; you can access books, magazines, newspapers, on-line services, college catalogs, and professional journals to add to or eliminate jobs from your list of possible careers

Labor Market Research 101

Okay, okay, okay. We can hear your questions even before they've tumbled out of your mouth. *"How in the world do I go about finding an exciting job or career? Can I do it while I'm working? What if I find a job I like, but it requires a degree I don't have time to get? Or what if I think I'll like it, but after I get it, I find out it's not a good fit?"* Our clients have asked us these questions and more. They are all very valid questions. We intend to answer them in this chapter and the next three, so hang in there. Our career-transition process is not theoretical verbiage; we learned what worked for us and our clients, and have stuck with it.

In this chapter, you'll start with a grocery list of careers you're interested in and by the end of chapter six, you'll have whittled your list down to what you want and what you can get. That's the heart of labor market research. Many of our clients have certain career fields in mind that denote glamour or prestige to them, but, in reality, are nothing like what they imagine. For example, one of

> "An objective without a plan is a dream."
> Douglas McGregor

our clients told us, *"I've always wanted to be in public relations."* She thought it was a spectacular field to be in. But public relations isn't a *"party"* field. It actually involves writing, which isn't especially glamorous. Unless you have the ability and personality to sit down and write for hours, you don't belong in public relations.

Labor market research gets you in touch with reality. It'll put your perceptions to the test. You may eliminate careers you thought were right for you and consider others you never really thought about before.

We liken the steps of labor market research to the rings of a bull's-eye. Each step gets you closer and closer to the middle—to making a career decision. The first steps are relatively easy. They provide a comfortable avenue for researching different jobs and careers. But each step requires more commitment on your part to the process, and this sometimes means leaving your comfort zone to zero in on the career or job you want. But it's the only way you'll get to your target.

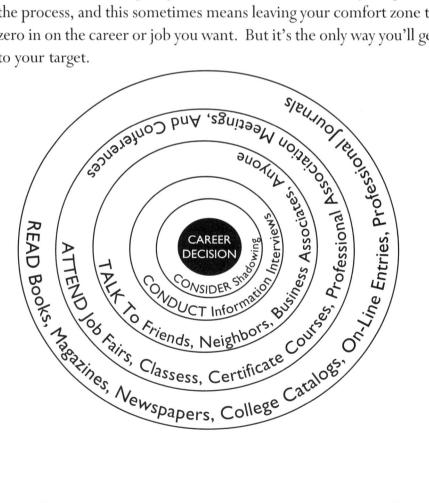

Tackling the Time Issue

Before we take you through the steps of labor market research, we'd like to discuss what the process requires in terms of time. We've touched on the time issue in the previous chapters. Now we'd like to tackle it for you.

Throughout the first two chapters, we've had you look at the immediacy of your need to make a career transition. Some of you feel the need strongly. You're very dissatisfied with your present career, you're experiencing adverse physical symptoms, or a layoff either has occurred or is imminent. Others of you feel an urge to change, but it's not so pressing. You're unhappy, bored, curious, or just looking ahead for another career, be it a retirement career or otherwise.

Whatever your situation, you're probably becoming aware that a successful switch will take time and effort. There are no shortcuts; you will have to find the time if you want to make a career change. That's why the current job or career you're in has to be manageable in terms of time. If you're working eighty-hour weeks, putting in six or seven days a week at your job, the reality is that you don't have time to change careers anytime soon.

By changing careers, we don't mean finding a new job in a career you think you'd like. We mean finding a new job in a career you know you'll like. That's the whole gist of labor market research—in reality, it can save you a lot of time. We want to save you the time and pain of jumping into a new career that might not be right for you. If you're in your twenties, you might have the time to try out new careers by actually working in them. By the time you're in your thirties and forties, however, that's no longer a viable option. So, while labor market research can save you time that you might have wasted by jumping into the wrong career, it still requires an investment of time on the part of anyone who wants to do it right.

"The best time to look for a job is when you have one."
Anonymous

This is a Catch-22. We've had a number of clients who were literally tied to their organizations. They were working too many hours—and had become too important to their organizations or departments—to even think about making a career transition. Of course, these clients asked us, *"Should I quit my job?"*

Well, career counselors never tell people to quit their jobs. We showed them the process, and they made their own decisions. Some of our clients who had very demanding jobs did decide to quit. They realized that the career-transition process went beyond time-management techniques. No amount of juggling time or their schedules would have allowed them the extra time to complete the process. But they had enough money in the bank *(or they found a "hold-me-over" job)*, they knew it would take at least three to six months, and they worked at it every single day.

Maybe you have a demanding job, but you don't have the option to quit. Perhaps you're a single parent. You can still go through the career-transition process. It'll just take longer. The average amount of time it takes to get through the process is one year; it could take you two or three years. However, it is doable, so don't give up. Many of our clients who didn't feel an immediate pressure to change careers also opted to travel the road to a career transition very slowly. The path stays the same regardless of when you start and when you finish. Take it at your own speed.

One of our clients, Taylor Mirasma, a young mother with two sons, left her marriage and the family-owned business she had worked at with three months' income. "I knew, from your advice," Taylor told us, "that I would really have to apply myself. I worked at finding a new career like it was my job. I did it every day, and I did it wholeheartedly." Using the techniques and strategies we taught her, Taylor discovered that instructional design was the field for her. She was interested in writing training manuals. "In the language school

I owned with my ex-husband," Taylor said, "I used instructional design skills, so I put together a portfolio of my work. Then I began interviewing and landed a job in instructional design at a large aerospace firm." In three months, Taylor closed down a business, got a divorce, moved, took care of two children, and found a new career.

Reading Is More Than Meets the Eye

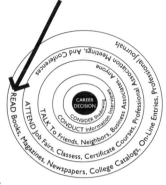

This first, easy step toward making a career decision involves research through reading. We encourage you to read books about specific careers, to explore new careers on-line, and to leaf through newspapers, magazines, college catalogs, and professional journals. It's a wonderful way to start dabbling in career information. In fact, we often advise our clients to clip *(or photocopy)* articles of interest and start files or scrapbooks of careers that appeal to them.

In this step, you're reading for interest. You're sampling careers in the broadest sense of the word. It's like checking out clothes in a magazine before you try them on and buy them, or it's comparable to reading personal ads before dating a number of people and choosing a mate. Even if you have a good idea of what you'd like to do, keep yourself open. Don't restrict yourself by narrowing down your choice to one or two job titles before you do this step.

You're reading to explore new careers, to uncover more information about one you're already thinking about, and to gather data that will allow you to make a good career decision. This data is always changing. That's why reading is on the outside of the bull's-eye. Printed material becomes dated fast. So while it's a valuable, easy way to learn about different careers, it's not the last word on the subject.

"Begin difficult things while they are easy... A thousand mile journey begins with one step."
Lao Tse

> "Read the want ads to get a clue about what's going on out there. But don't expect them to solve your job dilemma."
>
> Anonymous

Reading about specific careers clues you in on whether or not you want to pursue those careers. It answers question number one of labor market research—Do I desire to do this? Sometimes the information given also covers pay and demand, the other two questions, but remember that your answer to question number one is of utmost importance. Read to uncover your response to that question.

Check out the newspaper want ads

As a source for actually getting a job, want ads have a low success rate. Many of you already know that. However, reading want ads in a major newspaper tells you so much about the world of work. You don't need to do it every day. Just grab yourself a cup of coffee on Sunday, sit down, and read the want ads.

What will reading the want ads tell you? If you're looking for a specific job, you'll want to note what it's called and what section it's in, because those will vary. You'll want to look at job descriptions and see if they appeal to you. You also can sometimes uncover salary information, and you'll get a feel for the market and who is hiring.

Don't answer any of the ads right now. We just want you to see what appeals to you. If something does, rip it out, and put it in your file. And if you can't find anything much, don't be discouraged. Most jobs aren't advertised. But you just may find something that sparks your interest.

Cruise through college catalogs

Most of you live in a community that has one or more community colleges, as well as state colleges and universities, both public and private. The catalogs these institutions publish often offer a wealth of information about different careers. Take advantage of these catalogs. Call and ask for them to be sent to you.

What you want to do is to start looking through these catalogs for courses that pique your interest. You are not making any decision about enrolling in anything; however, the course descriptions will tell you much about what you like. If a course description does not appeal to you, most likely neither will the career.

In the next chapter, we'll give you more information on actually taking classes and courses. But for now, we just want you to see what interests you. You can access information from catalogs published for two-or four-year degree schools, extension-course catalogs, and community-service catalogs. Use whatever is available to you.

> *Mark Trelange, one of our clients who was an engineer for a large aerospace firm, was fully aware that his job was in jeopardy. "The administration was changing and defense money was being cut—these were all clues to me that I had better find something else to do," Mark said. He got hold of a major university catalog and asked himself, "What else would an engineer be able to do? I don't want to get another degree." Mark was willing to take additional classes, but he didn't want to spend years reeducating himself for another field of work. "Through reading that catalog, I found out about the field of waste-management disposal. I could use my current skills in this new field. Of course," Mark said, "I followed the rest of your advice about labor market research, but eventually I transitioned into the field of waste-management disposal, a career for which there was a great demand."*

Peruse professional journals

If you have some idea of a career field you'd like to join, consider reading a journal that relates to that field. Most of them have at least one journal that talks about the field. Major libraries usually carry these journals, so you can check them out before you subscribe.

For example, if you think you want to be in training and development in a corporation, you can go to any major library and read the *Training and Development Journal*, published by the American Society for Training and Development. If you're interested in advertising, read *Ad Week*. If human resources appeals to you, read the *Personnel Journal*. If sales and marketing seems to be up your alley, peruse *Sales and Marketing Executive*. And if you're interested in general business management, read *Fortune* magazine.

You don't need to read every article. But you need to sit down and see what the profession is talking about. If you're not interested in what you're reading, it's a clue that you might not be interested in that career field. Reading professional journals is an easy way to eliminate a career field.

Of course, you don't have to understand everything that's in the journal; the authors may use jargon you are not familiar with. But if you're not interested in the issues they're talking about, you can cross it off your list of possible careers.

If, however, in reading this journal, you find yourself interested in the career field, the journal will give you:

◆ jargon
◆ issues that people in this field talk about
◆ a list of conferences and conventions that might be coming up
◆ ideas for questions that you can ask people in this field for when you take the next steps of labor market research

This first step of labor market research can be started immediately. All you have to do is open up a newspaper or go to the library or access journal entries on-line. Start reading what's around you. It's safe, quiet, and non-threatening even to introverts. But it's not something you do only once. You must do it continually; you must constantly read and search for new information about new career fields, whether you make a transition within the next six months or the next six years.

Summary

A career transition can be completed by anyone, if enough time and energy are allotted to the process. If you're too busy to do more than think about a career change, you might need to see what you can do to free up the time it takes to make a successful career transition. If that's not possible for you, be assured that a career change can be made; it will just take longer. So be patient. In fact, even the time-challenged person can easily take advantage of the first step of labor market research. It involves reading— books, magazines, newspapers, professional journals, on-line entries—anything written that relates to careers that appeal to you. Begin reading now. You'll be that much closer to a career decision.

"Nothing comes from doing nothing."
William Shakespeare

Chapter 4 Key Points

- 🔑 The second step of labor market research requires that you attend job fairs, classes, certificate courses, and professional association meetings and conferences to get you closer to your career decision

- 🔑 Don't lose hope if you never earned a college degree or you don't want to get another one just to change careers; many new careers can use the skills you already have or only require a certificate

- 🔑 Even if attending classes, association meetings, and job fairs only allows you to eliminate careers, it still puts you ahead of the game

Stepping Out

4

Careers don't quite come alive on paper. While reading is a valuable part of labor market research, this next step involves getting out of your seat and attending events that open up doors to new career opportunities. It does require more commitment on your part than reading does, but it will also get you closer to your career decision.

Attendance Is the Name of the Game

This next ring closer to the bull's-eye requires more work on your part. However, attending meetings and classes shouldn't be that uncomfortable even if you are an introvert, because you'll be part of a large group. You can even go to the meetings and say nothing. But if you're interested in networking and meeting people who can assist you, you will need to think of a way to appropriately introduce yourself at these group meetings, so that other people can understand why you're there and how they can help. If you've read *Marketing Yourself and Your Career*, you'll already have a marketing script prepared. If you haven't, create a suitable introduction. It will make the events we ask you to attend more meaningful.

You need to inform people of your skills and ask for their help. To do so, you should create a self-marketing script that is both confident and informative. Most of our clients need help coming up with one. For example, a teacher looking for a career change wouldn't want to say: *"I'm a teacher, but I'm a really hard worker. I'm bored with my job, but I don't know what I want to do next or what I can do."*

Instead, that same teacher could say something like: *"I'm an educator and trainer who's looking for a new challenge in the business world. I'd like to use my program-development skills, my communication skills, and my training skills to train employees in various areas. Could you tell me who you know who does that? I'd like to meet and talk with them."* Notice how direct and specific this introduction is. The contact now knows how to help this individual, and is impressed with his or her confidence and knowledge of skills. If you work on and create your own meaningful introduction, the people you meet will be more willing and able to help you through your career transition.

Seeking Out Job Fairs

"You rarely get the part by attending a job fair. But it's a great way to practice your audition skills."
Linda Schilling

One of the first events you may wish to attend is a job fair. We ask our clients to approach it the same way they do want ads. Job fairs rarely result in an actual job. Probably less than two percent of the people who attend a job fair get a job offer from one. So please do not go to a job fair with the expectation that you will walk out of there with a brand-new job. On the plus side, however, job fairs do offer a tremendous opportunity to do your labor market research and to practice your self-marketing skills in a safe environment.

At a job fair, you will learn what jobs are available, who is hiring and recruiting in large numbers, and often what those jobs pay. A word of caution, though—not every job available at a corporation will be represented at the job fair. However, you will get a feel for a particular corporation and its environment.

We advise our clients to get dressed in their business best and have their resumes ready. You may even be given a brief interview at the job fair. That's why we tell our clients that it's great practice at self marketing. Go with the idea that you are window shopping. It's not a waste of time if you want to see what's out there and need practice presenting yourself.

Attending Classes and Certificate Courses

You may also want to attend classes and certificate courses you have found in the catalogs you've been reading. Whenever we bring up this topic in workshops, participants usually ask us about the need for getting a college degree. Some career fields obviously demand a college degree or more. There's no way around it. Depending upon which career you choose, you may need a bachelor's, master's, or even a doctorate.

You might be unaware, however, that some career fields have no hard-and-fast rules about required college degrees. For example, most people in human resources inside a corporation have degrees, but by no means do all of them have one. There's no governing body that says you have to have a college degree if you're in human resources. So, two of the questions you'll be asking in your labor market research is what kind of training and education is required, and what kind of training and education do most people have in this career field you're interested in.

> "Education will not simply be a prelude to a career, but a lifelong endeavor."
> Maud Barkley

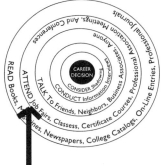

Many people do not get a four-year college degree, especially if they didn't get it between the ages of eighteen and twenty-two, because it requires too huge of a time commitment for the payoff. They have jobs, families, other responsibilities, and have no interest whatsoever in giving up eating and sleeping to get a degree. Others don't like theoretical learning, they don't have a long enough attention span, or they have no tolerance for subjects they're not interested in.

> *One of our clients, Marie Bronson, was a tarot-card reader at private parties. Before that, she was an administrative assistant at a printing and advertising business. "Working as a tarot-card reader helped me see that I had a gift of gab, a good sense of humor, and a way of capturing audiences," Marie told us. "I didn't have a college degree, but I persuaded a training and consulting firm to hire me without it. Most people in training and development have a college degree or an advanced degree." Marie learned corporate training with the consulting group and wanted to move on, but she was still worried about her lack of a college degree. Although she was very intelligent, she was unmotivated about returning to school. "I went on an interview to become a sales trainer, and I got it, again without even having the typical four-year degree a trainer usually needs." Since then, Marie made an additional move to another company—a major equipment manufacturer—and she is now the national sales training director. She has hundreds of people under her and has yet to get a college degree.*

If you don't have a four-year degree and find yourself in one of these categories, you can either forgo the idea or consider a couple of different options. You might become motivated to start or complete a degree if your corporation holds out a promotion or the offer of a better job. And, if they offer a tuition-reimbursement program, so much the better. Or you might discover that the career field you always wanted to be in does demand a degree, and you really want to pursue that career field. A word of advice: if you do decide to get a degree, you might try to find a private college geared toward adult workers. Their schedules and classes are usually more flexible.

The classes and certificate courses we encourage our clients to consider are typically found in the community-service catalogs or extension-course or continuing-education catalogs of colleges and universities. What you will find in these catalogs are one-day classes and certificate courses specific to certain careers. Many schools provide one-day classes in a variety of career fields.

A participant in one of our workshops, Ken Galbrahns, was interested in travel. Ken took a one-day course—called "Careers in Travel"— at a local college. "The course told me all the different things you could do in the travel industry, what training was needed, what money you could expect to make, and the different opportunities in the field. The instructor even helped some students write their resumes," Ken told us. "This class was worth its weight in gold. I was still interested in travel as a career, but if I hadn't been after the class, I would have only been out fifty-nine dollars, not thousands of dollars and a year or two invested in long-term training." Ken decided that the job he was interested in was that of a tour guide. "A tour guide goes on vacation with a group of twenty to twenty-five people and baby-sits them while they're on vacation. Travel is the number one growth industry in the world, and tour guides are in great demand," Ken said. "It also pays well enough. So I answered my DPD—Desire-Pay-Demand— questions." Having taken that one-day class, Ken worked on his resume, contacted travel agencies all around the world, and got a job as a tour guide.

Some fields, however, are more complicated. You can't take only a one-day class and find yourself in a new career field. But there are a number of certificate courses that don't require a whole new degree. The advantages of certificate courses have appealed to quite a few of our clients. Some have taken certificate courses in fund raising, accounting, career counseling, public relations, quality assurance, and purchasing, among others. Almost every field has a certificate these days.

What are the advantages of getting a certificate?

1. It's less time consuming. It doesn't take four solid years to get one. *(They're typically seven to eight courses that can be completed in one year.)*

2. It's less costly than a college degree.

3. You only learn a body of knowledge that pertains directly to the career field you're interested in.

4. Certificate classes are taught by people who work in the field during the day and teach at night. The classes, therefore, are action-oriented and practical.

5. You can have more than one certificate. *(One university we know calls it "career insurance.")* Most people don't have time to get more than one degree. They can, however, get more than one certificate.

6. Certificates allow you to try on a career, because many colleges and universities have an open house before the semester starts and they make you take the introductory course first. If you don't like it, you don't have to continue.

> *A participant in one of our workshops, Carlie Mason, worked for a large organization that was going through a major reorganization. "We were told that many people were going to lose their jobs," Carlie told us. Meanwhile, a job in human resources became available on the job-posting system. "Sixty people applied for the human resources position, but I got it because I had taken the time to get a certificate in human resources." The certificate was by no means the only reason why Carlie was selected for the position, but it increased her chances for getting the job.*

Giving Professional Associations and Conferences a Try

One of the quickest and easiest ways to get a picture of whether or not you'd like to be in a particular field or career is to attend a professional association meeting or conference related to that field. Most professional associations allow newcomers who aren't already a part of the field to attend meetings and conferences. However, a few elite organizations do not. For example, if you're considering becoming a doctor, you won't be welcome at an American Medical Association meeting. You have to be a doctor. Not every professional association provides easy access to career changers, but most do.

So how do you find a professional association that's connected to a career field you're interested in? Many local cities and communities have listings in the business section of their major newspapers of where the professional associations are meeting. Typically these are listed on Mondays. Also, in some communities, individuals have compiled a directory of professional associations. Check and see if one is available at your local library.

If neither of these options provide leads, do not give up. Ask your local librarian for a listing of the national headquarters of professional associations. Or, if you're already reading the association's professional journal, look in there for the phone number or address. Then write or call the national headquarters of the professional association you're interested in. They'll give you the name and phone number of the local chapter.

> *One of our clients, Martin Ludlowe, was a high school teacher interested in finding a new career. Martin had both good teaching and program-development skills. "I was torn between training and designing training programs," he told us. Martin attended two professional association meetings. One was ASTD, the American Society for Training and Development, where people in the training field gather. The other was STC, the Society for Technical Communicators, an association for technical writers. "Visiting these two association meetings gave me a good snapshot of the two different fields," Martin said, "and helped me make a decision fairly quickly. As a more introverted person, I felt that I fit better with the members of STC. They were quieter, more analytical, and interested in technical subjects. I found my home at STC." Attending these association meetings helped Martin uncover his true career interest.*

Is discovering the career for you as simple as attending meetings? Yes, it can be that easy. Many of our clients either choose careers or eliminate career choices that aren't right for them by attending professional association meetings. At an association meeting, you'll find fifty or sixty people who represent that career field. They have a collective personality. If you've ever gone to a professional association meeting, you'll know what we're talking about.

If you don't think there's a difference in personality among people who work in different career fields, attend an accounting meeting at lunch and a sales meeting at dinner. There's a huge difference. We're not saying that all the same personality types gather in the same fields, but there is a trend toward similar interests and behaviors. You might feel alien in one group, and at home in another.

While you are doing some initial career shopping, we suggest that you attend as many professional association meetings as you can find that are interesting to you. Obviously, you won't just join any group. But if you have some career options in mind, start looking for professional groups related to those career options and begin shopping.

Attend a meeting, sit back and gauge the crowd, and determine whether or not you fit in. Although you may decide not to go back to some groups for a second meeting, one or two may strike you as associations in which you'd like to become more involved. In fact, if a group does appeal to you, consider joining it.

Professional associations are often more than willing to help career seekers and people who are changing careers, especially if you're willing to volunteer your time and effort for the association. Most associations have memberships for people who aren't in the field yet. They view it as their mission to help people get into the field. We advise our clients to join and begin volunteering for different committees.

"Professional groups like shoppers, especially if they're eager to buy."
Anonymous

One of our clients, Vic Horning, was a high school principal who decided he wanted to make a career change. He shopped around and visited different professional associations, and finally decided that he felt most comfortable at ASTD (American Society for Training and Development) meetings. "After I joined, I immediately volunteered for a committee," Vic told us. "I enjoyed the work, and I invested my time and enthusiasm. A year later, one of the board members asked me to run for office. I actually ran for and won a position on the ASTD board before I was in the field. I still worked as a principal." But the association saw him as a valuable volunteer who was willing to give his time. Shortly after he was appointed to the board, another member took note of him at a meeting and told him about a job opening at her company. "I now work for a large, national restaurant chain in their training and development department. And to what do I owe my success? The simple process of getting involved in a professional association."

If you're unsure of how to take full advantage of attending professional association meetings, read the following checklist. If you follow the suggestions listed, your labor market research will be productive.

Association Networking Checklist

Before the meeting

1. Decide what to wear so that you will project a professional image.
2. Set a goal of how many people you want to meet and talk to about their careers.
3. Bring your business cards.
4. Think of ice breakers or conversation starters and stoppers.
5. Be prepared with an introduction and self-marketing script.

During the meeting

1. Mingle with the members and ask for their business cards.
2. Pick up any pertinent literature, such as an association newsletter.
3. Tune in to your overall reaction to the group *(its members, their personalities, the meeting format, etc.)*.
4. Try to pick an interesting table of people to talk to.

After the meeting

1. Write down your reaction to the group.
2. Think about and list what you have learned from this meeting. Are you still interested in the field?
3. List any volunteer opportunities that would help you.
4. Think about any key themes or issues important to the field. Are they of importance to you?
5. Think of whom you met. List the names of those with whom you intend to follow up.

Professional associations also host local, regional, and national conferences. As you start to get involved in a group, you'll learn about these conferences. They also are of tremendous benefit, because they provide yet another view of the career field.

> *One of our clients, Anne Rescome, was a secretary who was interested in meeting-and-events planning. She hooked up with the local chapter of Meeting Planners International (MPI) and discovered that they were hosting the national conference the next month in lieu of their monthly meeting. "I registered for the national conference," Anne told us, "slapped on a name tag, and attended a number of the sessions. I loved it. I liked the people, their conversations, and the information in the sessions. At the end of the evening, I gathered in the bar with many of the members, ordered a soft drink, and met people." Anne actually got a job lead in the bar that evening. She went through the rest of the steps in labor market research and eventually ended up in an entry-level job for a tour company, planning their events.*

While many people attend association meetings and conferences and find what they've been looking for, others attend the same meetings and discover that the field is not for them. It is definitely worth the money you pay to attend these meetings or conferences, even if you decide you never want to return. It's all part of labor market research. You rarely happen upon Prince or Princess Charming on the first go-around.

We like it when clients come back and tell us what they didn't like about a meeting or a conference. If you can voice what you don't like, then you have a clearer picture of what you want. You should be excited about what they're talking about. If you're bored out of your mind, then you know it's not for you. And if you can eliminate a career option, then you're one step closer to finding your ideal.

Summary

Labor market research comes to life when you step out and attend job fairs, classes, and professional association meetings. You get a taste of what different career fields are like, and you can either add them to, or strike them off, your list of potential careers. Whatever your decision, you're learning more about what you like and don't like in a career. As we tell our clients, you have to muddle through a lot of information before you can make a clear career decision. But it's the only way to ensure the right choice.

Chapter 5 Key Points

- 🔑 For some people, talking to strangers is a big step out of their comfort zones; however, talking about careers is a tremendous way to uncover careers you never knew existed and to eliminate careers you know you'd never want to pursue

- 🔑 You have to learn to start talking to everyone anywhere about careers; it's the best way to build your contact base

- 🔑 If you're an introvert, think of yourself as a *"career investigator"* whose role it is to learn about the careers of others

Talking Your Way to a Good Career Decision

5

Yes, we're going to nudge you out of your comfort zone in this step of labor market research. Unless, that is, you love to talk to people. If you do, you'll find it easy and enjoyable. If you don't, we hope to show you the immense benefits that can result from talking to anyone and everyone about potential career fields.

If you are interested in making a career change, you can't know too many people. Not only do you need to start talking to the people you know, but you also have to start thinking about making new friends and contacts. One of the things that gets many of our clients in trouble is that they don't have nearly enough contacts when they need to make a sudden change *(e.g., when they are hit with a layoff)*. Or they haven't kept up with the contacts they have made.

We're not saying that you need to have lunch with your contacts on a continual basis. If that were the case, that's all you'd be doing. No, by keeping up, we mean sending them little notes, an article of interest you came across, Christmas cards, and/or giving them a quick phone call every now and then. In other words, do something to let them know you're still around before you need something from them.

Talking your way to a good career decision means you must be open to talking to everybody. In this step, you will certainly run into a lot of careers that you don't want to try. But that's part of the process. You just need to ask, listen, and then later determine whether or not you'd pursue that particular career choice. If you wouldn't do it even if it paid a million dollars, you'll be able to eliminate it from your list of potential careers. You will always learn something by listening to people talk about their career fields.

What If You're an Introvert?

If you're an introvert, you may be saying to yourself, *"This isn't a good technique for me. I think I'll stick to reading about careers, and maybe I'll attend a meeting or two. But I won't start getting into other people's business."* Perhaps that's what you think, but we're not going to let you off that easy. This isn't an optional step. You have to become a career investigator and find out what other people do for a living.

You may run into people who don't want to talk about their jobs or careers. And, certainly, you must pay attention to body language and cues that let you know that others are not open to talking. Most people, however, do want to talk, especially about their most favorite subject—themselves. That's why this step is not difficult, even if you are an introvert. You're more likely to experience problems getting out of the conversation, not into it. When most people start talking about themselves, it's hard to get them to stop. They'll talk because you're showing interest in them, giving them verbal cues that you're listening, being polite, and because you'll be asking key questions, which we'll let you in on soon.

Most of our introverted clients find that they can do this step if they are given a role. So we give them one—that of a career investigator. We tell them it is their job to talk to people, figure out what they do for a living, and decide if it is something they would also like to do. And they fill the role extremely well. They might not be as enthusiastic about it as extroverts would be, but they do it competently.

Where, When, and How Do You Start Talking?

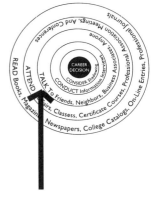

We'll be giving you an exhaustive list pinpointing where you can talk about career options. But to start you thinking, consider anywhere and everywhere you go. We tell our clients to broach the career subject in grocery store lines, in your doctor's waiting room, at your kids' sporting events, on a plane, at a company softball game, at a wedding, or at a retirement dinner. You get the idea.

Everywhere you go, you will have mini career conversations with the people you come in contact with. After an ice breaker, you can say, *"So, what do you do?"* As your contact describes his or her job or career, you prime the pump with statements, such as, *"Oh, really? How did you get into that?"* and *"Did you get formal training for that position?"* If you're interested, you might ask the demand question: *"Is there a demand for what you do?"* And if there's a demand, you can approach the pay question by saying something

"Men who try to do something and fail are infinitely better off than those who try to do nothing and succeed."
Lloyd James

like, *"If I were to consider a career in this field, what salary range would I be looking at?"*

A participant in one of our workshops, Jill Guenser, was flying to Denver and struck up a conversation with her seat partner, Louise, an attractive, well-dressed woman in her sixties. Jill and Louise talked about the weather for a minute, and then Jill asked, "What do you do?" Louise told her that she was a personal shopper for some of the wealthiest women in the world. "I travel all over the world," Louise said, "buying them clothes and then delivering the clothes. I get to travel to all the design houses in Europe." Would you be able to find this career in some book? Hardly. Jill didn't pursue it, but if she were interested, she could have looked into becoming a personal shopper for one of the major department stores.

But what if you discover, after hearing a description of the career, that you aren't inspired by it? Perhaps it's not appealing to you. Well, you can stop the conversation at any time by changing the subject and moving on. If the answer to your desire question is *"no,"* you aren't obligated to answer the pay and demand questions.

If, however, you are even somewhat intrigued by the career, ask the pay and demand questions. The answers will tip you off as to whether or not you want to follow up with a much longer interview, which we will describe in the next chapter. So if the answer to all three of the questions is *"yes,"* get the business card of the person you are talking to. In case the person does not have a business card, carry yours at all times. Give one of yours, and then write down the name and phone number of your contact on your card.

It is imperative that you always carry your business cards with you. You don't want to lose track of a valuable contact. One of our clients did just that at a wedding reception. She never got the name and number of the lady she was conversing with. And, because the bride and groom didn't know who the guest was, our client lost out.

"Career conversations can be as long as or as short as you like. If you're bored, back off."

Anonymous

Look at the following list of ideas on where and how to socialize to find out about potential career fields. It should stimulate some thoughts about where you can begin talking to others about careers.

Creative Connecting for Career Information

1. If you live in an apartment or condo, visit the pool to meet your neighbors.

2. If you are a teacher, have your students write a report about what their parents do for a living. Contact the ones that interest you.

3. Attend your high school or college reunion.

4. Join your college alumni association, obtain a roster, and attend the meetings.

5. Get to know the other parents who attend your kids' activities, such as soccer, Little League, ballet lessons, etc.

6. Take a one-day class or a tour from a community college to meet fellow class members.

7. Join the board of a nonprofit organization and get to know your fellow board members.

8. If you need sales contacts, determine what you would like to sell and contact people who purchase these products (*i.e., contact your doctor if you're interested in selling pharmaceuticals, or try a toy store owner if you'd like to sell toys, etc.*).

9. Ask your hairdresser or manicurist to introduce you to their clients who are in career fields that interest you.

10. Go through your personal address book and write a letter to everyone you know. Tell them what career fields you are interested in, and ask for contacts. Send them a self-addressed envelope or follow up with a call.

11. Talk to professionals you may work with who have a large client base *(e.g., your doctor, financial planner, accountant, dentist, etc.)*. Tell them what career fields you are interested in and find out whom they know.

12. As you are working out at the gym, be sure to initiate conversations with the people around you.

13. Call all the people you have worked with in past jobs and careers to tell them what you are doing. Ask for contacts.

14. Go to the local golf or tennis club for lunch and talk to people.

15. Go to a major shopping center and talk to as many customers as you can.

16. Attend city council meetings to meet people who are busy and active in the community.

17. Attend the opening of a new exhibit at your local art gallery or museum to meet a variety of people.

18. Put a notice in your church bulletin, telling people in your congregation what career fields you are looking at. Give them your phone number so they can contact you.

19. If you are a nurse, contact former patients and their families to tell them about your career transition, and inform them about whom you would like to talk to.

20. If you sell real estate, hold an open house and survey everyone who comes to look at the house.

21. Go out to breakfast, lunch, or dinner as often as you can afford to, and sit at the counter to meet the other people who sit there also. *(Be sure to target upscale restaurants and areas.)*

22. Call up old boyfriends/girlfriends and tell them what you are looking for.

23. Shake the family tree and locate distant relatives who might be contacts for you.

Places and Events I Already Attend

Now list some of the places and events you already attend, and come up with new places you can go to talk about career options. You should be able to create a good-sized list.

_____

_____

_____

_____

_____

_____

_____

_____

_____

_____

_____

_____

_____

_____

_____

_____

_____

New Places I Need to Go

_____

_____

_____

_____

_____

_____

_____

_____

_____

_____

_____

_____

_____

_____

_____

_____

_____

*"Things do not change:
we change."*
Henry David Thoreau

Use these lists and start talking to people. In addition to a box of business cards, you'll get career information you couldn't have gotten any other way. Certainly, you'll talk to scores of people with jobs that you'd rather not touch. But you'll also uncover some opportunities you never knew existed. And one of those careers may end up being your future career.

> *A client of ours, Renee Beckett, attended a golf tournament in Palm Desert and conversed with a lady behind her in the bathroom line. "I started by talking about the weather," Renee said, "and then I noticed she had a beeper on and a phone in her hand. So I said, 'You must be at work.' She was." In fact, Renee discovered that this lady was the head of the golf tournament. She was totally in charge of the golf tournament, and she spearheaded three every year—one in Palm Desert, one in Scotland, and one in Florida. "She makes about $75,000 a year," Renee told us. Such a job would never be advertised and probably never written about it. Renee got her card and asked her permission to follow up later.*

Any Objections?

Some of you will look at your lists of places to go and can hardly wait to get started. Others of you are loathe to write down one place, because you don't want to talk to people. Please get over it. This kind of talking to people speeds up your career-change process exponentially. However, if this is not your natural way of operating, and meeting strangers is not your favorite thing to do, take it slower, one step at a time, and don't try to do everything on our list.

Many of the clients we had to encourage to start talking found it relatively easy once they tried it. They'd meet a person in a class or talk to a neighbor down the street and discover that it wasn't difficult to get good career information. The first encounter usually gave them the confidence to continue.

Because you will always be in some sort of career transition, you should get used to talking to others about their careers. You'll get better at it the more often you attempt it. People who do this consistently and do it well are never without job leads, never without contacts, and never without a place to go. If you're interested in that type of security, you need to be interested in doing this.

People like to hire people they know and have met, and enjoy making others they know aware of job openings. Forty-nine percent of the people who get hired in the United States get hired through a friend, a neighbor, a relative, or a contact they met. That's nearly half the world of work. Have we convinced you yet? Meeting other people and talking about careers is not a haphazard route toward a mediocre career decision. It's a clear path toward a career decision that fits your needs.

One of our clients, Rick Starmont, was an unemployed aerospace engineer who knew he had to work hard at finding a new career. "I always had an interest in the stock market," Rick told us, "but I had never thought about it as a career. However, based on your advice, I decided to talk to individuals at the discount brokerages I frequented. So I started talking to the brokers in the office. Before I knew it, I was hired as a broker." Rick showed an interest, started talking and interviewing these individuals, and found out that he was great at sales when it dealt with a technical subject he was interested in.

Summary

Not everyone is comfortable talking to friends, acquaintances, and strangers about career decisions. However, we have found it to be one of the best ways to gather information on careers and to make contacts that can help you eventually land a job that matches your desires and abilities. Try it out. Once you do, it will become easier and easier. And don't forget to always have your business cards on hand. You don't want to lose touch with the contacts you make.

Chapter 6 Key Points

- 🔑 Information interviews and shadowing, both techniques used in this last step of labor market research, are reserved for careers that appeal greatly to you

- 🔑 Call to set up an information interview with the people whose careers interest you the most; make sure you follow the interview etiquette and ask as many pertinent questions as you can

- 🔑 As an optional technique, shadowing can provide you with a hands-on look at your potential career; we suggest that you use it whenever possible

A Picture's Worth a Thousand Words

6

All of the different techniques and strategies that we've given you so far should have helped open your eyes to the very large world of work. Undoubtedly, you've seen things you'd never want to do. And, hopefully, you've also come across careers you would enjoy. Because now it's time to follow up with some of the people you've met in professional association meetings or conferences, instructors you've had in certificate courses, or the people you've met on ski lifts, in grocery stores, or at parties—the ones whose business cards you've obtained.

To actually find out whether or not the career choices you've identified are for you, you'll have to follow this last step in the labor-market research process. You'll be conducting information interviews with the people you've met and shadowing them while they're at work. Doing these things will bring the picture of the career or careers you're considering into sharp focus.

Getting Your Questions Answered with Information Interviews

An information interview is an interview to solicit information about the career field you are seriously considering. It is not—absolutely not—a job interview. We can't stress this point enough. The purpose of the information interview is to get you as close to the career field as you can without actually taking a job in it. The other technique in this step, shadowing, is a method you can use to bring you even closer to your possible career; that's why we reserve it for last. But information interviews are not optional, and they are absolutely critical to making a successful career decision.

With information interviews, we're getting towards the center of the bull's-eye. We tell our clients that they should go from warm to hot in this step—that if their career choice is right for them, their excitement should increase by the time they finish their information interviews. You do not conduct information interviews on careers you have already eliminated. You only proceed with careers that appeal greatly to you.

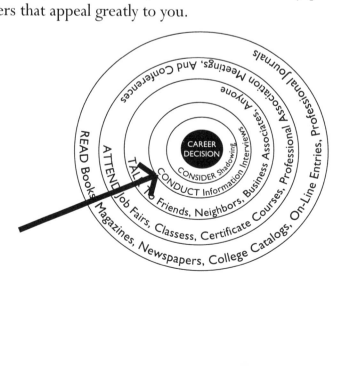

What do you get out of it?

> *One of our clients, Ben Ogden, was worried about where he was going to fit into the world of work, because he was in his sixties. "I started out thinking about training and development," Ben told us, "but then I discovered that my age was an impediment. I had the skills, but I felt that most people in the field were much younger than me." We suggested fund raising to him. "No," was Ben's first response. "I'm not into bake sales and begging for money." But he did attend the National Society for Fund-Raising Executives, and he met some people in planned giving. Planned giving is an offshoot of fund raising, where you discuss leaving money in your will to an organization of your choice. Ben started to become interested in the field. "Through the association, I made some contacts, and I conducted some information interviews," he said. "In the information interviews, I learned that there was a lot I liked about planned giving. And through the contacts I made, I landed a job in planned giving for one of the major universities." It was a natural career for Ben. He was charming, he talked to people his age, he believed in the university, and he raised more money than anyone on the staff. In addition, he made a lot of money—somewhere in the six figures. "But it was the information interviews," Ben told us, "that spurred me on to get into the field. Without them, I never would have made the leap."*

Why should you conduct information interviews? Well, the information you gathered from that person you met at a party, in your dentist's waiting room, or in a class isn't enough on which to base a major career decision. You need to sit down with the people you've met in the environment in which they work and size up what they have to say about the career field. In so doing, you'll get to see your potential career field in all its dimensions.

> "Research on careers takes time. A quick chat in a ticket line won't fill you in on all the nitty-gritty details."
> Anonymous

We realize that you've already questioned individuals about their careers. But in an information interview, you'll get to ask more pointed questions, and the detailed answers you receive will allow you to make a rational decision. So, get out the business cards of the people whose careers interest you, call them up, and set a specific time to talk with them about their careers at the actual job sites.

How do you go about it?

Now, don't worry. We're not going to leave you stranded, wondering what you should do, what you should wear, and what you should talk about with your contact. We give our clients etiquette guidelines and a list of questions to ask.

What do we recommend in terms of etiquette for information interviews? Look over the following list.

Information-Interviewing Etiquette

1. Wear professional, business-like clothing, unless some other type of dress is required or normal.

2. Set up the interview at your contact's absolute convenience.

3. It is appropriate to carry a note pad, briefcase, or portfolio for carrying your questions and paper to jot answers.

4. You may take notes, but not to the extent that it inhibits interaction with the person interviewed.

5. Watch the time to make sure you're not going past what has been allotted.

6. Thank your contact profusely when you leave.

7. Write your contact a thank-you letter once you get home.

8. Once you've made your career decision, follow up with your contact and tell him or her what you decided to do and what happened to you. It gives your contact a sense of completion.

"That sounds good," you're probably commenting to yourself. *"But what on earth do I say,"* you ask, *"other than 'Tell me about your job'?"* Well, have we got a list of questions for you. In fact, if you look at the following list, you'll see that we've provided you with more than enough questions to ask. It is an exhaustive list. You probably will not need to ask all of the questions, but you should know the answer to most of them by the time you've completed your information interview.

Interview Questions to Test Your Ideal Job

General Information

1. Name *(You should know this; however, if you only know the first name of the individual you're interviewing, ask for his or her last name.)*
2. Title
3. Company
4. Years with company?
5. Previous positions held with the company?
6. How did you join/form company?

Additional Questions to Ask

7. Could you describe what one of your typical days is like?
8. What do you like least/most about your current position?
9. What are your future plans?
10. How does one get training and experience for this job/field?
11. What is the role of a college education in this company and for this job?
12. What other kinds of opportunities/positions exist within this company? What are the chances for advancement?
13. What opportunities are there for women in this company?
14. Are there professional organizations and journals in this field?
15. Whom do you know with a job similar to yours in another environment?

Questions to Assess the Environment

16. How much flexibility do you have in defining your job and in scheduling and pacing your work?

17. To what degree are elements of your job consistent and predictable *(job parameters, relationships with co-workers, mobility, advancement)*?

18. What is the company's philosophy about its products, service, and employees?

Questions to Assess Interaction with People, Data, and Things

19. Do you deal primarily with people, data, or things?

20. What is the degree and nature of the interaction with people *(alone, one-to-one, small or large groups, teamwork, team member, outside contact)*?

21. To what degree do you have time to yourself to plan and work?

Questions or Aspects to Consider Regarding Your Interests and Issues

22. Ask yourself about the tone, mood, and feeling of the organization. Can you identify with and support their philosophy, product, and service?

23. What is the process for hiring, firing, and evaluating employees?

Questions about Working Style, Preferred Skills, and Preferred Roles

24. What kinds of activities are required for this position *(creating, implementing, managing, marketing, problem solving, etc.)?*

25. What skills do you need to be successful in this job?

26. What roles do you play in this company and in this position?

27. Analyze to what degree you *(the career searcher)* can get your pay-off and the greatest satisfaction from working in a position or career such as this one.

Questions to Ask Regarding Essentials

28. If I were to consider a career in this field, what salary range could I expect?

29. What are the typical benefits of this company, this position, and/or this career field?

30. What is the company policy regarding travel?

Questions Specific and Relevant to This Field

Add questions that relate specifically to this career field.

_____

_____

_____

_____

"If the description of a typical day at work leaves you wishing it were atypical, you need to move on."
Anonymous

The question that will probably get you the most information is number seven: Describe what one of your typical days is like. Let us assure you that most people will tell you that they don't have a typical day. You need to respond with *"Of course not. Tell me about yesterday."* Having them describe a typical day tells you more about that career field than almost any other question you see on this list. So pick and choose these questions, asking the ones that are most important to you, but do not—under any circumstance—skip number seven.

> *A client of ours, Amanda Hastings, went on an information interview in human resources. Like many people, Amanda thought she wanted to be in human resources because the job would have a great deal of people contact. "Well," Amanda told us, "it does and it doesn't." She interviewed a person who was an HR generalist in a small company of about three hundred employees. This person played all the HR roles. "When my contact described her typical day," Amanda said, "I discovered that the job was over 50 percent paperwork and data. The information interview brought the career into my view. I learned what I did and did not want out of human resources." Amanda did choose human resources, but she went with a much larger company and entered the area of human resources called employee relations, where you solve employee problems. "My new job has far more to do with people than the job an HR generalist does."*

What's the best approach?

Even if an information interview helps you discover that you don't want to be in that career field, you have not wasted your time or energy. Wouldn't you rather eliminate that career at this point than get into it and find out you don't want to be there? The information interview can also help you pinpoint what you do like and don't like about a particular career. In so doing, you can steer yourself toward a position in that field that more closely fits your desires.

> "Wise men learn by other men's mistakes, fools by their own."
> Anonymous

That's why it's important to conduct more than one information interview. Often the same job title has very different duties and responsibilities based on the size and type of company. That's where question number fifteen comes in. You'll be asking for names of other contacts who hold similar positions in different environments. If you're at all interested in the career, schedule at least two or three information interviews. By going on more than one interview, you can identify exactly what you're looking for in a position and in a company.

The more information interviews you conduct, the more you will begin to see how valuable they are. Conducting information interviews allow you to:

1. Get information about the career field you're interested in. You'll be able to see whether or not you want to pursue that particular career.

2. Learn more about the field itself. You'll start to pick up jargon, acronyms, and important issues in the career field you're considering.

3. Try out many different environments. You'll find out which environments appeal to you.

4. Start making contacts in the field. You'll be able to use those contacts when you're going after a job.

The more information interviews you go on, the more practice you will get in presenting yourself. So, in addition to learning if the career field is for you, you will be preparing yourself for job interviews. We also tell our clients to consider those they interview as possible contacts for future jobs. It just may be that the person you interview for information can help you get a job.

One of our clients, Michelle Glenn, a special-education teacher, had attended several professional association meetings before coming to the conclusion that training and development was the field for her. Michelle became active in ASTD, attended their conferences, read their journal and newsletter, and began information interviewing people in the field. "During my first five information interviews," Michelle told us, "I said very little about myself. I just asked the questions you gave me. By interview number six, I knew much more about the field and began to do more talking about myself." Michelle stopped conducting interviews after the tenth one. "I made sure to be pleasant during all the interviews and to write thank-you notes after they had been completed. Then, when I finally decided that I wanted to be in training and development, I wrote to the people I interviewed with, sent them my resume, and let them know I was now looking for a job. I turned the information-interview people into contacts." Michelle also applied for jobs advertised in the ASTD newsletter, but it was through one of her information-interview contacts that she eventually got her first job as a trainer.

Shadowing for Good Measure

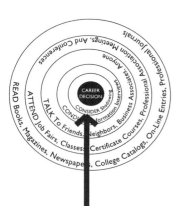

For those of you who really need to see a potential career in action, we've got one last technique. It's called shadowing. Some people never do it, and other people must do it. Shadowing is spending a minimum of two hours and a maximum of half a day with someone in a career field you think you'd like to join. In shadowing an individual, you actually watch him or her work.

For some of our clients, a chat across a desk doesn't cut it. They have to see, smell, and touch the career. It's never a bad idea to shadow someone before you make your career decision. But some people need to make shadowing mandatory, while for others it's optional.

Of course, some jobs are far easier to watch than others. It's probably less important to shadow a computer programmer than a police officer, because it's easier to grasp what exactly a computer programmer does in the course of a day. The predictability is fairly high.

If, however, you're going to go into a career such as sales, you should consider shadowing. In fact, most major organizations that hire sales personnel have them ride along with a sales person for a day. So, if you're interested in sales, shadow before the job interview. You'll learn whether or not you can get in and out of your car as often as your contact, you'll see the customers your contact interacts with, and you'll know what actually goes on during a typical day in the field.

> One of our clients, Robin Pullman, thought she wanted to be in fund raising. "I had done several information interviews," Robin said, "and I understood that it wasn't just asking people for money. But I still needed to see the job in action." She shadowed a fund raiser, Paul, for half a day. The two of them went to a breakfast meeting in the morning as Paul made a speech about his organization. They went back to his office, and Robin listened as Paul called board members to remind them to phone the major donors they were in charge of. Then Paul had a meeting with his staff about a 10k run they were putting on the following month. And, finally, Robin joined Paul and a corporate sponsor for lunch. "At the end of my half day of shadowing," Robin said, "I knew I wanted to be in fund raising. It had so much variety and so many different people to interact with. Paul never once had to personally solicit money from anyone. But I wasn't convinced about the field until I actually shadowed."

We know many a nurse and many a teacher who wish they had shadowed before they had gotten into those fields. We tell our clients to seriously consider shadowing. If you feel you need this additional step, take it.

Another of our clients, Marguerite Bentley, had done several information interviews in the career field of patient relations. Someone in patient relations is an ombudsman, or a troubleshooter, for the patients in a major hospital. "I really liked what I had heard in my information interviews," Marguerite told us. "I had the skills required for the job, there was a demand for it, and the pay was more than adequate. But I still thought I should watch someone in the position." So Marguerite shadowed Betty, a woman in patient relations. The first hour or so went well. "Betty first dealt with some patients who had billing problems," Marguerite explained. "Then some other patients needed help understanding what they were to do at home after they were discharged. Betty took care of them, too. But then Betty was paged and asked to come to a floor in the hospital where pandemonium reigned. Two women were having a gigantic fist fight out in the hall. Previously unknown to each other, these women were both married to the man who was dying in a nearby room. Betty had to break up the fight and arrange a visiting schedule to ensure the two families never met." Marguerite decided she didn't have the temperament to deal with such crises. However, she did eventually end up working in a hospital, arranging children's programs for young inpatients. It was a much calmer career field, and it fit Marguerite's personality better.

Summary

We certainly realize that conducting information interviews and shadowing contacts requires effort on your part. But both provide tremendous opportunities for actually determining whether or not a career is for you. Why do you think we call our career-transition process almost risk-free? We couldn't afford to have our clients change to a career they didn't like. We'd never get recommendations that way. Information interviewing and shadowing enabled them to get as close to the career as they could, short of actually getting a job. Besides, conducting information interviews also provided a practice ground for their self-marketing skills and helped them strengthen their contact base. Use these techniques if you want to see your potential career field as it actually is, there's no better way to get a crystal-clear picture of any career.

"Well——I imagine you have a few questions of your own."

Chapter 7 Key Points

🔑 Labor market research leaves you with more information than you know what to do with; we suggest you keep a career journal to write down your reactions to the careers you are researching

🔑 In addition, you need to find a career confidant—a person who supports your career change and can provide you with feedback

🔑 To stay on course, come up with a plan of action for each career option, and commit to completing at least one item on your action plan every week

🔑 You'll have to sort through lots of information to come up with the career that's right for you, but you can do it if you persevere

🔑 Keep on doing labor market research; then, whenever you or your organization changes, you'll be prepared

Pulling It All Together

7

In the preceding chapters, we've supplied you with plenty of research ideas, techniques, and strategies. However, you will need some way to process this information and to start making career decisions for yourself. If you get good at meeting people, attending professional association meetings, and conducting information interviews, you will gather a tremendous amount of information. You'll need a way to deal with this information overload and a plan to keep you on course as you progress through each step of labor market research. Stick with us; we'll show you how to do it.

Keeping Tabs on Your Progress

In our experience, one of the best ways to manage the mounds of information you'll be gathering is to keep a journal of your progress. At the end of every career encounter—whether it involves a stranger you met on an airplane, a professional meeting you attended, a class you took, a magazine article you read, or an information interview you conducted—as soon as you are able, you should immediately write what you liked and didn't like about what you heard, read, and/or learned. Writing down your reaction to the careers you learn about will enable you to sift through the information you receive and pull out what's important.

It may seem like extra work, but it's necessary work you do now to save time down the line. Think about it. If you happen to talk to five individuals about their careers in the course of a week, how do you expect to remember all of the details and your initial reaction to each of the careers? And what happens when, ten weeks and fifty mini career conversations later, you're having a hard time recalling who said what, when?

Don't worry; we're here to walk you through the process of writing about your career investigations. We learned quickly what was important to remember, because we listened as our first clients complained about what they had forgotten. As a result, we advised the thousands of clients who followed after to keep a journal.

The following journal entries belong to one of our clients, Phil Barber. Phil graduated with a business degree, and *"fell"* into a purchasing position with a large medical-device manufacturer. *"It was a great first job,"* Phil told us the first time we met him, *"but I'm growing bored and restless. I don't think the 'fast track' is in purchasing."*

We asked Phil about the opportunities within his own organization, and he admitted that there were quite a few. *"I'd like to get ready for both the opportunities inside my company,"* Phil said, *"and any outside that might interest me."* We walked him through the career-transition process and explained all about labor market research. Then we handed Phil a copy of *Unlocking Your Career Potential*, and asked him to read it.

> "Be like a postage stamp; stick to one thing until you get there."
> Josh Billings

Based on his assessment of his abilities, skills, and desires, Phil decided that he'd like to look at both sales and marketing as possible careers. *"I enjoy interacting with people,"* Phil said, *"but I also love data. I think either sales or marketing would be a good choice for me, because they are "fast-track" careers, and they'd afford me more independence and autonomy."* Phil started his labor market research. Later, he told us that keeping a journal was essential. *"It helped me sort through what I was learning."* Read through some of his initial entries.

Phil Barber's Journal

March 30th

Attended my first meeting of the Sales & Marketing Executives. Regardless of the title, this is definitely a "sales" group. It was a little awkward at first, but I met a new member, Jim Berchley, at the sign-in table and we hit it off. I realize if I want to be in sales, I'll need to be more at ease meeting lots of new people. I enjoyed the meeting and the people I met. I'm going to follow up with Jim and have lunch. He sells a fairly technical product that has some appeal to me. Already, just from dinner conversation, I can see I probably want to sell a fairly complicated product and not a service. Too intangible for me!

We needed to introduce ourselves to the whole group. I was nervous, but realized I just needed to give my prepared marketing script. Thank goodness I had gone over it right before the meeting. It worked like a charm. Everyone really liked my line about wanting to be in sales and call on people in purchasing, something I would definitely know how to do!

April 5th

Had lunch with Jeremy Rumbley, a product manager at my own organization. Luckily, I got his card two months ago when we both ended up in the same training class at work.

Jan and Jane said information interviews would be easy because people like to talk about themselves. How true! Jeremy loves his job and was a wealth of information. He spoke highly of the certificate program I'm looking at, too. Product management is quite data-oriented, but I liked everything I heard. I'll definitely need more information interviews. Jeremy recommended a friend of his from school. He's with a pharmaceutical company. I'll call him next week.

April 10th

Just got back from the Open House for the Marketing Certificate Course at the local university. I met five of the instructors and was impressed with all of them. They work in marketing for a variety of companies and teach at night and on weekends. I could see myself doing that! I have until the first of June to enroll for the introductory course, but I'm pretty sure I will. I collected all the instructors' business cards and I'll be following up later.

April 21st

I took Sue Bellows out for coffee this morning. She has been calling on my corporation for about 5 years now. I asked her to keep our meeting confidential, which she was glad to do. I liked what she had to say about her job, and the money is certainly decent. But somehow I'm still not sure about sales. I've asked Sue if I can ride around with her one morning next week. I'll have to take a vacation day, but that's okay. I think I'll learn a lot more by watching her.

April 27th

Just spent the day with Sue on her sales route. We started at 7:00 a.m. I knew sales people spent a lot of time in their cars but I didn't appreciate how organized you need to be. We made 5 calls before a 1 p.m. lunch. Three of the calls were to old customers and two were "cold calls." Those would definitely be the most difficult for me. I left her after lunch, but she said she had four more calls to make and then phone calls and paperwork yet to complete. I'll say this—sales reps earn their money! This shadowing technique is very, very helpful.

May 1st

I met with a marketing consultant, Ron Baldwin, today. Even though I couldn't be a consultant right away, it was good for me to talk to him and see the future. Ron held a variety of marketing positions before he went out on his own, so he was very helpful. He described a lot of different positions in marketing—most of which I qualify for right now. My "gut" tells me I would be happier in an office figuring out the marketing angles and letting the sales reps go out and sell.

Even though I feel I'm qualified for several marketing positions, I realize I still need to convince others. The first thing I'm going to do is enroll in the marketing certificate program. Then I'm going to start documenting my skills the way the Marketing Yourself And Your Career book described it.

It sure feels good to have a goal and know I'm not stuck in purchasing forever!

The next set of journal entries belongs to another of our clients, Julie Long. Julie returned to school in her thirties and got a degree in psychology. She then spent over twenty years in human resources. *"I'm looking for a retirement career,"* Julie told us at our first meeting. *"I can retire from my company in five years, and I'll have enough money to meet my basic expenses,"* she said, *"but I still want to work, if only part-time."*

We told Julie that she was smart for being so forward-thinking. *"You're doing your homework in plenty of time to reap the rewards of a retirement career,"* we told her. Julie decided to explore two opportunities that would allow her both to use her degree and to continue working with people. She opted for looking at becoming a professional mediator or deciding to return to school for her marriage-and-family counseling certificate *(MFCC)*. Because the second option would mean investing a great deal of time and money, she knew she should research both options thoroughly.

Julie, like Phil, found that keeping a journal of her progress helped her focus clearly on her labor market research. With Julie's approval, we've included some of her entries.

Julie Long's Journal

September 25th

I have read a couple of mediation books, and I am so excited about the concepts. I have always disliked the adversarial part of my human-resource career. I can see now as I look back that I have tried many times to play the mediator role between managers and employees.

October 3rd

I called the Mediation Center about the training program and have enrolled in the next class. I can't wait to begin.

October 10th

I wanted to wait to do my information interviews after I started my training, but I met a mediator at a professional group this morning. She is a divorce attorney who mediates when clients want a more peaceful solution. She loves mediating and is always sad when clients don't feel like they can get divorced without hurting each other.

October 14th

I've attended six out of the twenty-five hours of mediation training in the class I'm taking. I love this class and the ideas being presented. I'm beginning to think I would be a good mediator, although it is much more complicated than I originally thought. I'm glad the Mediation Center has additional training classes and some opportunities to observe. This is not something you can learn in twenty-five hours.

October 28th

I've completed the class and did a quick information interview with the instructor who mediates for corporations. He has said I could arrange to shadow him soon.

November 4th

I've done my information interviews with the attorney and the divorce mediator. I haven't shadowed my instructor yet, but I think business mediation is the direction I want to head. The attorney handles a lot of contract mediations (which bore me), and the divorce mediation seems too emotional for me.

November 20th

I observed the first three-hour mediation of a manager and his employee. I'm not ready to mediate, but I was very comfortable with the situation and the discussion.

I am very interested in pursuing this option further. It's such a great extension of what I have been doing. Once I get more training, I could probably talk my boss into letting me set up a pilot program right here. I would love to consult in this field. My instructor seemed to have a really good schedule and lots of flexibility.

I will also explore getting my MFCC, but the additional education and hours of interning makes it less feasible and certainly less appealing.

Use Phil and Julie's entries as a guideline when you start your own journal. However, do feel free to make your journal as personal as you'd like. Some of our clients found it helpful to explore their feelings in their journals; others kept them more business-like. Whether your journal looks more like a list or a diary, you'll find that writing down pertinent facts and feelings helps you sort through the massive amounts of information you'll be receiving. We've provided worksheets in the next chapter that can function as your career journal; or, if journal writing comes easily to you, simply use the worksheets as a springboard for your more expansive thoughts and feelings.

Choosing a Career Confidant

Another method for sorting information that we suggest to our clients is to choose a career confidant, a person with whom you can share your career reactions and impressions. Your career confidant should listen carefully and give you feedback that allows you to come to some sort of conclusion about what you're doing. However, we offer a word of advice: choose your career confidant carefully. It is best, of course, that your confidant knows you. A career confidant can't be a stranger. However, he or she also can't be somebody very close to you.

If you choose a spouse or even a co-worker, please understand that these people may have an agenda for you. By that we mean that they may or may not be thrilled about you leaving your present job and/or changing careers. Find a friend or co-worker who is enthusiastic about your change and who has no agenda for keeping you where you are.

Unfortunately, the whole world doesn't love a career changer. In the career-transition process, you will meet many wonderful people. But you will also, on occasion, meet people who don't want you to change. Whenever you talk about changing or discuss a meeting you attended or a new career you uncovered, they will try to encourage you to stay right where you are.

It happens. Think about the other major changes you've made in your life. There have always been people who didn't want you to make that change. It's the same with a career change. Perhaps a spouse is concerned about the salary you'll make if you start over in a different field, or a co-worker doesn't want you to leave the organization you're at.

Whatever the reasons behind their concerns, acknowledge them but remain true to yourself. Let these people know that you value their opinions, but that you're still going to make a change. That's why your career confidant needs to be somebody who will back you up; otherwise, you'll get discouraged right away.

Two of our clients, Denise Maldon and Carrie Fairfax, met at a professional association meeting—Women In Sales. "Both of us knew we were there to gather information and do labor market research," Denise said, "so we decided to form a career-change club of our own, with just the two of us as members." Together, the two decided that sales was the career field for them, and both chose to join Women In Sales. "We attended the meetings together," Carrie said, "we talked about the people we met, and we shared the names of our contacts for information interviewing and shadowing. Through the support we received from each other, we made the transition into sales." Carrie and Denise found sales jobs in different companies. "But the process for both of us was much easier because we had each other," Denise shared. "A career confidant is a tremendous boost."

If you can find someone who is also going through a career change, so much the better. Oftentimes, you can find such a person at an association meeting. The exchange of information and ideas can be very helpful. It's like people who lose weight together. They are more motivated and excited because they have the support of another in the same predicament.

In addition to bouncing your career information and impressions off a career confidant, you should also bounce them off your career checklist from *Unlocking Your Career Potential* or your *"Career Temperature"* self assessment from chapter one of this book. Otherwise, you'll have no context in which to place the information you've gathered. You'll go in circles unless you have a reference point. So, whether or not you've come across a career article, attended a meeting, talked to a contact, shadowed an individual, or conducted an information interview, you need to debrief by writing in a journal or talking to a friend. How does this new information fit with what you decided you want out of a career?

Yes, we realize you may discover that what you thought you wanted has changed. For example, you may have decided upon 30 percent people contact, until you got out there and started networking and switched to 60 percent. Your knowledge of what you want often changes when you get in touch with the real world of work.

"Procrastination is the thief of time."
Edward Young

A word to the wise: things do become muddier before they get clearer. As you start your labor market research, you're going to collect a bunch of data. It may take you a while to see through it all, to zero in on what you want. But we have seen, with all the thousands of clients we've worked with, that if they got out there, did their labor market research, and bounced it off their confidants and their previous assessments, they eventually discovered what it was they wanted to do. They had to sort through piles of information, but they finally settled on their vision. Perseverance was the key for them, and it will be for you also.

Coming Up with a Plan of Action

The career-transition process works better if you set goals for yourself. Yes, we know that you may be doing your labor market research while you are currently working. But we suggest that you do something for your new career weekly—attend a meeting, take a class, or have one information interview. Get out and work on your future at least once a week.

We recognize that time is an issue here. If you aren't currently working, you should be doing something every single day. Why? Because you're in more of a hurry to change careers. Labor market research should be a priority for you. If you have a job and other responsibilities, we understand that it's not realistic to ask you for a daily commitment. But you should be able to fit a weekly career activity into your schedule.

"To avoid criticism, do nothing, say nothing, be nothing."
Elbert Hubbard

We advise our clients to come up with a plan of action for each career option they choose, so that they don't have to sort through the different labor-market research activities each week. You can do the same. A career action plan will save you time and frustration. You'll have your activities written out for you, and you'll check off each planned activity after you've accomplished it. Phil Barber and Julie Long, the clients who shared their journal entries with us, also agreed to let us print their action plans.

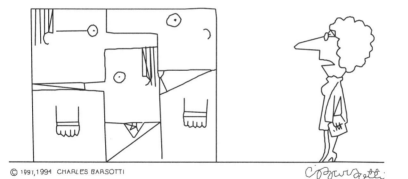

© 1991, 1994 CHARLES BARSOTTI

*"Gentlemen, can we stop networking long enough to
get some of the work done around here?"*

Career Action Plan

Client: Phil Barber

Career Option: Sales

Information To Read:	**Completed:**
Sales & Marketing Executive Journal	March 26

People To See/Call:

1. Joanne Barnes (met at church)	April 2
2. Dr. Wilson (for pharmaceutical rep referrals)	April 9
3. Jim Berchley (met at Sales & Marketing Executives)	April 15
4. Tom Simmons (2nd cousin; met at family reunion)	April 19
5. Sue Bellow (calls on our department)	April 21, 27

Group/Associations To Attend:

Sales & Marketing Executives	March 30

Possible Education/Training:

"Career In Sales"—one day class at local university	May 15

Other:

Purchase "Zig Ziglar" motivation tape

Career Action Plan

Client: Phil Barber

Career Option: Marketing

Information To Read:	**Completed:**
American Marketing Association newsletter	March 25

People To See/Call:

1. Jeremy Rumbley (product manager at work)	April 5
2. Ron Baldwin (marketing consultant)	May 1
3. Theresa Wright (met at AMA conference)	May 25

Group/Associations To Attend:	
American Marketing Association National Conference	May

Possible Education/Training:	
Open House for Marketing Certificate Program	April 10

Other:

Career Action Plan

Client: _Julie Long_

Career Option: _Professional Mediator_

Information To Read:	**Completed:**
Getting to Yes	_September 12_
Designing Conflict Management Systems	_September 24_

People To See/Call:

1. _Joe Brown (attorney who also mediates)_	_October 29_
2. _Sue Johnson (federal mediator)_	_November 2_
3. _Debbie Bellows (divorce mediator)_	_November 8_

Group/Associations To Attend:

Society of Professionals in Dispute Resolution (Spider)	_November 8_

Possible Education/Training:

Mediation Certificate (25 hours)	_October 28_

Other:

Use the following form to write your own plan of action. In fact, we encourage you to photocopy it, since you'll need one for each career option you choose. Fill them out; then store them in your career file or journal.

Career Action Plan

Career Option: _____

Information To Read: **Completed:**

_____   _____

_____   _____

People To See/Call:

_____   _____

_____   _____

_____   _____

_____   _____

Group/Associations To Attend:

_____   _____

_____   _____

Possible Education/Training:

_____   _____

_____   _____

Other:

_____   _____

_____   _____

The key to all this is the consistency with which you do it. So, even if you only do something once a week, you will eventually make a change because you are consistently and persistently working toward a goal. If you read this book and follow the steps of labor market research, you can't help but make some kind of change for yourself. It may be a major change, or it could be a minor one. But something definitely will happen if you stick with it.

> *A client of ours, Myra Beaton, worked as an engineer at a major computer company. She wasn't sure whether or not she wanted to leave the company, but she was getting a little bored with the projects she was handed. "I took your advice and began doing something once a week. I first did some reading. Then I decided to broaden my horizons by attending a professional engineering association," Myra told us. "I even got very involved and joined a committee. On that committee, I met a man who was working on one of the most exciting projects I had ever heard of." Myra started to talk to him about the details of the project, and discovered that he worked for the same company she did. "Through my contact with him," Myra said, "I made a change within my company and am very happy." She didn't know where her efforts were going to lead her, but she initiated a change, worked on it consistently, and her efforts led her right down the hall.*

"Everything comes to him who hustles while he waits."
Thomas Edison

Phil Barber spent three additional months making his career transition. He joined the American Marketing Association, and became active on a committee. *"I also enrolled in the certificate program,"* Phil said. *"I had just finished the introductory course, when Jeremy Rumbley, the product manager at my work, called and told me about a new opening in the marketing department."* Phil applied, along with several other candidates who had heard about the job through the job-posting system.

"I got the position," Phil told us. *"And, although there were several reasons why I got it, I credit three with giving me the edge I needed. One, I did my homework and learned as much as I could about the field of marketing. Two, I joined the American Marketing Association and enrolled in the certificate course. And three, I learned how to market myself, and I felt confident that I was the best candidate for the job."*

Julie Long decided to go into mediation for her retirement career. Because she still had more than four years remaining at her current job, Julie signed up for more classes at the Mediation Center, joined the Society of Professionals in Dispute Resolution, and took the initiative to start a pilot program in mediation at her corporation. *"My boss was very receptive,"* she told us in a follow-up call years later. *"And, in allowing me to add mediation to my work duties, he made my remaining time more enjoyable and gave me the added experience it took to start my own mediation consulting business once I retired. I'm so glad I took the steps to plan for my retirement career."*

Continuing Your Good Work

Please understand that labor market research is an ongoing process and should be done continually. If you land a new job or a new position inside or outside of your company, the process doesn't end. You won't need to make a huge commitment to labor market research, but you should always remain open to discussing and researching new careers. You never know when you might want to make another switch.

So don't pack this book away once you've made a change. Keep abreast of any changing desires on your part, take your career temperature on a regular basis, and ask yourself if you're still happy, challenged, and satisfied with your present career. Use the techniques and strategies in this book constantly. If you think of yourself as always in transition, always in search of the next best contract, then you'll always be ready whatever happens—whether you or your organization changes.

Carol Ipsen, one of our clients who was a language teacher, made a major career change. She became an instructional designer for a well-known restaurant chain. "I'm thrilled with the change," Carol informed us after she had made the switch. "I love my job. But I'll never forget what you taught me. I continue to do my labor market research. I attend association networking meetings every month, I have a card file of all my contacts, and I continue to update the file." Five years later, the restaurant chain moved, and Carol turned herself into an independent contractor. She now works as a consultant for other restaurants, doing their instructional design for them. "I went back to my card file and called up many of my old contacts," Carol said. Some had moved, but many didn't. And those I called welcomed me as a contractor and a consultant. Labor market research really pays off."

Summary

If you're at all interested in some sort of career change, sitting at home thinking about it won't do you any good. You have to get involved with labor market research. And, yet, as valuable as it is, all the labor market research in the world is useless unless you have some way to sort the information and relate it to your needs, abilities, and desires. We suggest that you keep a journal and that you enlist the help of a career confidant. Both methods will help you debrief the data you gather.

Then take what you've learned and see how it fits with what you want. If it's a match, you can forge ahead with that particular career field. Of course, all this does take commitment to the career-transition process, so we also advise you to come up with a plan of action. We ask that you choose to complete one action step every week, more often if you're currently out of work. And when you do change careers, keep your options open. Don't regard labor market research as a past activity. Continue reading, making contacts, attending meetings, and talking to individuals. Then, whenever you're ready to make another move, it'll be painless.

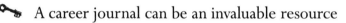

Chapter 8 Key Points

- A career journal can be an invaluable resource

- Some people find it difficult to start a journal without assistance; we suggest you fill out the provided worksheets to come up with ideas, to sort through new information, and to evaluate your progress

- Remember that your career journal doesn't have to look like everyone else's; create it to be an asset for you

Starting Your Career Journal

8

Some people take to pen and paper with great ease. Others stall in the face of writing paraphernalia, and still others freeze. We realize that some of our clients will only chronicle their successes and setbacks if we provide worksheets for them to fill out. Some of the material listed is taken straight from this book. We've just placed it in chronological order for you to consider.

You may choose to use the following pages as your career journal. Another option is to use this chapter to stimulate ideas, which you can then explore more fully in your own expanded journal. It's for your personal use to assist you in your career-transition process. Refer to pages 79 through 82 for several examples of our client's journal entries.

"History unrecorded results in lessons forever lost."
Susan Parker

Taking Note of Early-Warning Signs

Agree____ Disagree ____ 1. I start to feel anxious on Sunday afternoon, because I don't look forward to going to work on Monday morning.

Agree____ Disagree ____ 2. I experience one or more chronic physical symptoms, such as headaches, stomach problems, and/or backaches.

Agree____ Disagree ____ 3. On Sunday morning, I automatically reach for the funnies or the sports page, but then decide to check the want ads first.

Agree____ Disagree ____ 4. At work, I find myself constantly watching the clock.

Agree____ Disagree ____ 5. I feel like I'm on a treadmill that doesn't have an "*off*" button.

Agree____ Disagree ____ 6. At a work meeting, I seem to be less excited than anyone else in the room.

Agree____ Disagree ____ 7. I don't really care about any promotions at work.

Agree____ Disagree ____ 8. My "*give-a-rip*" level is low.

Agree____ Disagree ____ 9. I fantasize about doing something totally opposite from what I'm currently doing.

Agree____ Disagree ____ 10. I've started counting the years, months, and/or days until retirement.

Gauging Your Career Temperature

Apply each statement to your current job or career by placing a check mark in the appropriate space. If you complete this assessment on a consistent basis, you'll be much more in tune with your current level of job satisfaction.

1. Opportunity to use the skills I enjoy   ____Very Satisfied ____Satisfied ____Somewhat Satisfied ____Dissatisfied ____Very Dissatisfied

2. Demands work makes on my time   ____Very Satisfied ____Satisfied ____Somewhat Satisfied ____Dissatisfied ____Very Dissatisfied

3. A salary which reflects my contribution   ____Very Satisfied ____Satisfied ____Somewhat Satisfied ____Dissatisfied ____Very Dissatisfied
   to my organization

4. A benefits package that meets my needs   ____Very Satisfied ____Satisfied ____Somewhat Satisfied ____Dissatisfied ____Very Dissatisfied

5. Clothes and image that are required   ____Very Satisfied ____Satisfied ____Somewhat Satisfied ____Dissatisfied ____Very Dissatisfied
   for my job

6. Opportunity to interact with people I enjoy   ____Very Satisfied ____Satisfied ____Somewhat Satisfied ____Dissatisfied ____Very Dissatisfied

7. Quiet time to immerse myself in data   ____Very Satisfied ____Satisfied ____Somewhat Satisfied ____Dissatisfied ____Very Dissatisfied

8. Opportunity to grow and develop   ____Very Satisfied ____Satisfied ____Somewhat Satisfied ____Dissatisfied ____Very Dissatisfied

9. An environment that I enjoy going   ____Very Satisfied ____Satisfied ____Somewhat Satisfied ____Dissatisfied ____Very Dissatisfied
   to every day

10. Opportunity to apply my creativity   ____Very Satisfied ____Satisfied ____Somewhat Satisfied ____Dissatisfied ____Very Dissatisfied

11. The amount of status and prestige   ____Very Satisfied ____Satisfied ____Somewhat Satisfied ____Dissatisfied ____Very Dissatisfied
    attached to my job

12. The match between my value system   ____Very Satisfied ____Satisfied ____Somewhat Satisfied ____Dissatisfied ____Very Dissatisfied
    and that of my organization

13. Flexibility in setting my own schedule   ____Very Satisfied ____Satisfied ____Somewhat Satisfied ____Dissatisfied ____Very Dissatisfied

14. The long-term prospects of my   ____Very Satisfied ____Satisfied ____Somewhat Satisfied ____Dissatisfied ____Very Dissatisfied
    job and/or field of work

15. The challenges and learning opportunities   ____Very Satisfied ____Satisfied ____Somewhat Satisfied ____Dissatisfied ____Very Dissatisfied
    afforded by my job and/or field of work

Your response to this assessment is totally individual. That's why there's no answer key. You may be strongly satisfied with all points except one and still consider your *"career temperature"* to be cold. Or you may be very dissatisfied with four or five points and yet feel a great deal of warmth toward your career choice. So look at each of the statements and especially pay attention to those you marked *"very satisfied"* or *"very dissatisfied."* Do those have meaning for you? Are they important? If *"very dissatisfied,"* can you change them within your present career to increase your career temperature?

_____

_____

_____

_____

_____

_____

_____

_____

_____

_____

_____

Taking Care of the Time Issue

Labor market research does take time. In can take as little as three to six months if you tackle it full-time, or it can take you years, if your need is less pressing and you can't currently devote your wholehearted effort to it. The time issue, however, is a major one, and you need to be honest with yourself about it.

How much time can you devote to the career-transition process? List all the times you can and are willing to devote to it *(e.g., Tuesday evenings, every-other weekend, every day, etc.)*.

_____

_____

_____

_____

If your current career is already too demanding and also undesirable, would you consider a *"hold-me-over"* job? _____ yes _____ no

If yes, list the types of *"hold-me-over"* jobs that are available to you. Put a star next to those you seriously would consider.

_____   _____

_____   _____

_____   _____

_____   _____

Considering Possible Careers

As you conduct your labor market research, you will keep uppermost in your mind the following three key questions (*Desire-Pay-Demand*):

1. Does this job or field interest me?

   (*Do I want—or desire— to do this?*)

2. What does this job or field pay?

3. What's the demand for this career field, now and in the future?

List all the careers you are interested in.

_____	_____
_____	_____
_____	_____
_____	_____
_____	_____
_____	_____
_____	_____
_____	_____
_____	_____

Now ask the DPD questions for each of the careers you have listed. Put a star by the careers that satisfactorily answer the DPD questions. As you explore more careers, add to this list.

Reading, Attending, and Writing All About It

Which careers have you uncovered through reading?

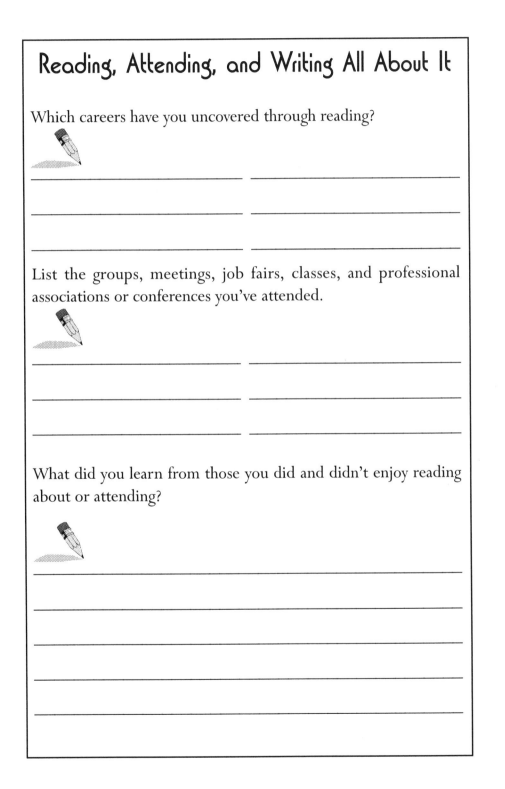

_____ _____
_____ _____
_____ _____

List the groups, meetings, job fairs, classes, and professional associations or conferences you've attended.

_____ _____
_____ _____
_____ _____

What did you learn from those you did and didn't enjoy reading about or attending?

_____
_____
_____
_____
_____

Tapping into Career Conversations

If you have yet to enter into career conversations, look at the following list and put a star next to the ideas that you would consider using.

1. If you live in an apartment or condo, visit the pool to meet your neighbors.

2. If you are a teacher, have your students write a report about what their parents do for a living. Contact the ones that interest you.

3. Attend your high school or college reunion.

4. Join your college alumni association, obtain a roster, and attend the meetings.

5. Get to know the other parents who attend your kids' activities, such as soccer, Little League, ballet lessons, etc.

6. Take a one-day class or a tour from a community college to meet fellow class members.

7. Join the board of a nonprofit organization and get to know your fellow board members.

8. If you need sales contacts, determine what you would like to sell and contact people who purchase these products (*i.e., contact your doctor if you're interested in selling pharmaceuticals, or try a toy store owner if you'd like to sell toys, etc.*).

9. Ask your hairdresser or manicurist to introduce you to their clients who are in career fields that interest you.

10. Go through your personal address book and write a letter to everyone you know. Tell them what career fields you are interested in, and ask for contacts. Send them a self-addressed envelope or follow up with a call.

11. Talk to professionals you may work with who have a large client base (*e.g., your doctor, financial planner, accountant, dentist, etc.*). Tell them what career fields you are interested in and find out whom they know.

12. As you are working out at the gym, be sure to initiate conversations with the people around you.

13. Call all the people you have worked with in past jobs and careers to tell them what you are doing. Ask for contacts.

14. Go to the local golf or tennis club for lunch and talk to people.

15. Go to a major shopping center and talk to as many customers as you can.

16. Attend city council meetings to meet people who are busy and active in the community.

17. Attend the opening of a new exhibit at your local art gallery or museum to meet a variety of people.

18. Put a notice in your church bulletin, telling people in your congregation what career fields you are looking at. Give them your phone number so they can contact you.

19. If you are a nurse, contact former patients and their families to tell them about your career transition, and inform them about whom you would like to talk to.

20. If you sell real estate, hold an open house and survey everyone who comes to look at the house.

21. Go out to breakfast, lunch, or dinner as often as you can afford to, and sit at the counter to meet the other people who sit there also. *(Be sure to target upscale restaurants and areas.)*

22. Call up old boyfriends/girlfriends and tell them what you are looking for.

23. Shake the family tree and locate distant relatives who might be contacts for you.

If you've already been involved in career conversations, what did you learn from them? How could you make them more productive?

Learning from Information Interviewing and Shadowing

Don't neglect these two very important techniques for helping uncover the right career for you.

List the people with whom you've conducted information interviewing and shadowing.

_____   _____

_____   _____

_____   _____

_____   _____

What did you learn from these encounters?

_____

_____

_____

_____

_____

_____

_____

_____

_____

Your Career Journal

Name: _____

Date: _____

Goal: _____

_____

_____

_____

_____

_____

_____

_____

_____

_____

_____

_____

_____

_____

Summary

If you are following the steps of labor market research and are using a career journal to further your progress, we're confidant that you're on the right track to a successful career transition. At times it may appear intimidating or too intensive, but it's also exciting, invigorating, and rewarding. Our clients take pride in learning what they really want from a career and in discovering new avenues for career growth. If you're willing to take the time and make an effort, a whole new world of work may be waiting just for you. We wish you the best in all your career endeavors!

Titles Currently Available

in the

Personal Growth and Development Collection

Managing Your Career in a Changing Workplace

Unlocking Your Career Potential

Marketing Yourself and Your Career

Making Career Transitions

Workshops

Dynamic and interactive in-house and public workshops are available from Richard Chang Associates, Inc. on a variety of personal, professional, and organizational development topics.

ADDITIONAL RESOURCES
FROM RICHARD CHANG ASSOCIATES, INC.
PUBLICATIONS DIVISION

PRACTICAL GUIDEBOOK COLLECTION

Available through Richard Chang Associates, Inc., fine bookstores, and training and organizational development resource catalogs worldwide.

QUALITY IMPROVEMENT SERIES

Continuous Process Improvement
Continuous Improvement Tools Volume 1
Continuous Improvement Tools Volume 2
Step-By-Step Problem Solving
Meetings That Work!
Improving Through Benchmarking
Succeeding As A Self-Managed Team
Satisfying Internal Customers First!
Process Reengineering In Action
Measuring Organizational Improvement Impact

MANAGEMENT SKILLS SERIES

Coaching Through Effective Feedback
Expanding Leadership Impact
Mastering Change Management
On-The-Job Orientation And Training
Re-Creating Teams During Transitions

HIGH PERFORMANCE TEAM SERIES

Success Through Teamwork
Building A Dynamic Team
Measuring Team Performance
Team Decision-Making Techniques

TRAINING PRODUCTS

Step-By-Step Problem Solving Tool Kit
Meetings That Work! Trainer's Kit
Continuous Improvement Tools Volume 1 Trainer's Kit
101 Stupid Things Trainers Do To Sabotage Success

VIDEOTAPES

Mastering Change Management**
Quality: You Don't Have To Be Sick To Get Better*
Achieving Results Through Quality Improvement*
Total Quality: Myths, Methods, Or Miracles**
   Featuring Drs. Ken Blanchard and Richard Chang
Empowering The Quality Effort**
   Featuring Drs. Ken Blanchard and Richard Chang
* Produced by American Media Inc.

HIGH-IMPACT TRAINING SERIES

Creating High-Impact Training
Identifying Targeted Training Needs
Mapping A Winning Training Approach
Producing High-Impact Learning Tools
Applying Successful Training Techniques
Measuring The Impact Of Training
Make Your Training Results Last

WORKPLACE DIVERSITY SERIES

Capitalizing On Workplace Diversity
Successful Staffing In A Diverse Workplace
Team-Building For Diverse Work Groups
Communicating In A Diverse Workplace
Tools For Valuing Diversity

TOTAL QUALITY VIDEO SERIES AND WORKBOOKS

Building Commitment**
Teaming Up**
Applied Problem Solving**
Self-Directed Evaluation**

** Produced by Double Vision Studios

EVALUATION AND FEEDBACK FORM

We need your help to continuously improve the quality of the resources provided through the Richard Chang Associates, Inc., Publications Division. We would greatly appreciate your input and suggestions regarding this particular book, as well as future book interests.

Thank you in advance for your feedback.

Title: _____

1. Overall, how would you rate your *level of satisfaction* with this book? Please circle your response.

    Extremely Dissatisfied   Satisfied   Extremely Satisfied

    1   2   3   4   5

2. What did you find <u>most</u> helpful?

    _____

    _____

3. What did you find <u>least</u> helpful?

    _____

    _____

4. What *characteristics/features/benefits* are most important to you in making a decision to purchase a book?

    _____

    _____

5. What additional *subject matter/topic areas* would you like to see addressed in future books from Richard Chang Associates, Inc.?

    _____

    _____

Name *(optional):*_____

Address: _____

C/S/Z: _____ **Phone:** ( ) _____

PLEASE FAX YOUR RESPONSES TO: (714) 727-7007
OR MAIL YOUR RESPONSE TO: RICHARD CHANG ASSOCIATES, INC.
15265 ALTON PARKWAY, SUITE 300, IRVINE, CA 92618
OR CALL US AT: (800) 756-8096